# Hustlers, Harlots and Heroes

## A Steampunk and Regency Field Guide

# Hustlers, Harlots and Heroes

A Steampunk and Regency
Field Guide

# Krista D. Ball

TYCHE BOOKS LTD.

# Hustlers, Harlots, and Heroes:

## A Regency & Steampunk Field Guide

Published by Tyche Books Ltd.

www.TycheBooks.com

Copyright © 2014 by Krista D. Ball

First Tyche Books Ltd. Edition 2014

Print ISBN: 978-1-928025-02-3

Ebook ISBN: 978-1-928025-03-0

Cover Art and Cover Design by Lucia Starkey

Interior Art by Stephan Lorenz

Interior Layout by Ryah Deines

Editorial by M. L. D. Curelas

Author Photograph by Krista . Ball

# Contents

# Acknowledgements

I'd like to thank Tyche Books and, particularly, my editor Margaret Curelas. A lot was happening in my life while writing this book. Margaret was incredibly supportive and understanding throughout this entire process, and for that I am very grateful.

Thank you to Jamie, Marie, and David, who helped iron out the kinks in this book. I probably would have joined the gin craze if it wasn't for Skyla, as well as everyone at Writers Cubed and the Diaspora Crew.

The staff at *Lois Hole Public Library*, as ever, was instrumental in obtaining the long list of books and journals I needed to research this book.

A special thank you must go out to all of my readers. I am ever humbled by how supportive you have been about this series.

Michael and Jacob somehow managed to get through this entire book with only being grounded three times. Clearly, I'm starting to mellow. Or maybe they're getting better at hiding their crimes.

As always, this book would not have been possible without Peter's unwavering support. I've decided to make an honest man out of him, if he'll have me. Any man who watches every single Austen adaptation and documentary with me is someone I want to keep around in my old age.

# Author's Note

So why did I focus on London in this specific age? I know that's a super specific era and location and it was a tough choice to make. My reasoning was that most of the stories I read set in this period, be they romance, fantasy, history, or science fiction, are either in London, or else someone eventually ends up in the city. This isn't just related to our steampunk vampire finishing schools, either. Off-world steampunk and dieselpunk books set in mythical new worlds often have a city or two resembling seventeenth or eighteenth century London. Regency romances often have an excursion to London for *the season*, where parties and dances were near-nightly events.

The Georgian and Victorian eras were an amazing time for innovation and social change in the Western world. In this period, we see slavery outlawed, the rise of women's rights, workers' rights, and the beginnings of a social safety net. That was all happening with technology chugging alongside.

I wasn't planning to solely focus on London; it just happened that way. I had planned to cast a wider net to encompass rural vs. urban differences, the country home, the urban slum, and the slave ships of Bristol and Liverpool. However, as I looked over the information in front of me, the books I've read, and reader feedback, I decided to narrow my focus to London.

London had a diverse mix of class, race, and even religion. It housed government and those who wielded great power. It had shops and clubs and theatre, and it also had dances proudly proclaiming Africans only. It had slums, poverty, and addictions. Alongside the rakes and the scoundrels, there were servants of both the domestic and the flesh. London was full of variety.

London was where Mary Crawford (*Mansfield Park*) enjoyed

the high society of the Haut Ton, Beau Monde, or le bon ton (whichever French term best suits your fancy for Regency London society). London was also where Miss Lydia Bennet went . . . sightseeing with George Wickham (*Pride and Prejudice*) when she ran away to elope. It's where Angel had his affair (*Tess of the d'Urbervilles*) and where Tom Jones learned he'd slept with his own mother (*Tom Jones*).

Many of the Regency romances I've read eventually have their heroines end up in London society at balls and house parties. Likewise, steampunk is often set there or set in a city that strongly resembles London.

Readers sometimes ask me if the world was really that way "back then," and my answer is sure, for a few people. Just like my life today is representative of a group of individuals in the world, likewise the experiences of dukes and duchesses are representative of their sphere.

If you are writing a rural set fiction, keep in mind London rules were different than country rules. I don't even mean rules of conduct, but the mundane every day. There were more strangers in London, more debt, vice, art, and culture. London was a metropolis and those from the city had a different way of seeing things than their country relations.

*"She is poor; she has sunk from the comforts she was born to; and, if she lives to old age, must probably sink more."*
- Jane Austen, *Emma*

# Introduction

I hadn't finished *What Kings Ate and Wizards Drank* when the questions began about the "next" book. Everyone had suggestions for what I should write next, from the history of sex to underwear, weapons to transportation . . . and the transportation of weapons! There was no stone left uncovered by the time my fabulous readers were done planning out my future writing career.

I spent some time asking myself if writers even needed another hybrid book like *What Kings Ate*. What wasn't already covered in writer guides and reader compendiums? Was there anything left?

I was re-reading Jane Austen's *Pride and Prejudice* at the time for an adaptation I was writing—*First (Wrong) Impressions*. I was diving into some of the internet forums, websites, and mountains of books concerning the history of Austen's time. A lot of conversations came up and the comments were rather surprising:

*Non-white people can't be in Regency novels.*
*Slavery didn't exist in Britain.*
*Slavery did exist, but it was over by the time Jane Austen was born.*
*Women weren't allowed to work "back then."*
*What I would give to live in Regency times; it was such a better time.*

The more I read, the more surprised I became. Authors proudly proclaimed that historical fiction didn't need to be based on actual historical details, while others were fighting tooth and nail to make their books as accurate as possible to the point of alienating their readers.

Some writers defended a lack of diversity in books by blaming reader expectations. Many readers were angry that books weren't accurate and others were angry when a book was accurate! Some wanted no diversity, some wanted lots of diversity, and still others said they had no idea about any of it and just went along with the flow.

Many people are genuinely interested in history. They might be writers, who are creating fiction steeped in reality. They might be readers, who want to know the bigger context of the stories they love. Others want to peek into the lives of people from another era.

So while that was all nice and dandy, did I want to crack open the books again so soon, looking at the myths of the 18th and 19th centuries?

That brought on the great internal debate and occasional Twitter argument. What was "steampunk" anyway? Was it really just a (white, rich, titled) woman bucking the system while eating cucumber sandwiches and wearing a bustle? Should Regency historicals be nothing more than pretty dresses and parties? Could a Napoleonic epic be anything more than brave men fighting the French, English, Spanish, and/or Russians in the gore fest of sword and musket?

I've read countless novels that were just as I described above and loved every word in them. Bernard Cromwell's Captain Richard Sharpe will always be my idea of a hero. A man's man, with his gutter manners and complete lack of respect for the chain of command; a lady's man who could make a petticoat lift on its own with a mere smile . . .

Sorry, where was I?

Romanticizing the past is very easy to do. The life of Lizzy Bennet (*Pride and Prejudice*) sounds relaxing when I have mounting deadlines. She can walk at her leisure, have time for crafts, have dinner with friends, and not even have to cook a meal for herself. But for the few Lizzy Bennets that did exist, there were plenty more servants who did Miss Lizzy's hair.

*Hustlers, Harlots, and Heroes* is for all of you out there who write Steampunk, who long for the glory days fighting against Napoleon, or who ache to save Tiny Tim and Oliver Twist. Whether you write Mr. Darcy fan fiction or daydream of being a governess and falling in love with a handsome, rich "widower" who happens to have locked his wife up in the attic (I won't judge), this book is for you.

You won't find many rich women of note, nor find many Earls and Dukes inside these pages. *Hustlers* is a quick and dirty field guide to help you write the people Austen left out, and Dickens talked about. The image of the genteel balls and the glorious gowns will be pushed aside. I'll explore the women of many backgrounds who scrubbed those ballroom floors, and the men who served and serviced those beautiful women.

This book is about the 99% of Georgian and Victorian London.

Many of you have told me that *What Kings Ate* was laugh-out-loud funny. There's no denying that me soaked in pig fat will be a lasting image. *Hustlers* won't be quite that funny. I can't laugh at the knowledge that a child could be sold for two yards of cloth the year Jane Austen was born. Or that men were hanged by the neck until they were dead and may God have mercy on their souls—for preferring the sexual company of men over women.

I hope to interject some eye-opening moments, like when I recreate Victorian soup kitchen recipes (not bad) or scrubbed my house in period clothes (hilarious).

As always, a writer's guide lies at the heart of this book. Whether you are writing about airships soaring across The Channel or a woman dressed as a man on the high seas, *Hustlers* will have something for you. I want to give you, the inventor and creator of your own mystical world, the tools to add conflict, drama, and realism into your story.

For those of you who plot mayhem for your Steampunk heroines, there will be plenty of ideas that go beyond the typical cogs, wheels, and steam. I hope to present you with challenges and questions to push your stories. I often provide the tough questions for you to ask your heroes.

Don't worry because the dashing Regency bucks won't be left out! I'll guide them past the working ladies of Covent Garden, giving them plenty of pointers along the way. Lovers of naval battles and land battles will find plenty of information on how to bring diversity to their armies for a realistic flair.

As with *What Kings Ate*, the best way to use *Hustlers* will be to view this book as the first rung on the ladder and not a definitive work. This is a beginner's guide; an introduction to another world often left out of the etiquette guides. My goal is not to answer your questions, but to create a hundred more.

Please feel free to run away with any of the story prompts and ideas. If you do that, I'd love to hear about it!

Of course, *Hustlers* isn't just for writers, even though it's a writer's guide. If you're in love with Major Richard Sharpe (*hubba hubba*), laughed at Mrs. Bennet, or dress up at fan conventions as a steampunkress, you're my kind of people. The entire reason we writers create worlds is because of readers. We write these stories for you to enjoy. I wouldn't dream of leaving any of you out of this adventure. You are the reason we get up the morning, stay up late at night, and drink too much cheap gin.

Ok, not all of us drink gin and once you get to that section, you might not either!

## The Lay of the Land

*Hustlers* will take you on a journey into the poor homes of the everyday worker. I'll show you their homes and meals. We'll do a tour of the dreaded workhouse and talk about salaries, bills, and expenses. We'll talk about the unique challenges that women and children faced in a world that required their work, but didn't treat them as equals. A chapter is also devoted to food, and several recipes and menus will be described for the culinary adventurers. Because, really, what's a book by me without a chapter on food? I'll also dive into charity and the social security net of the eras, as well as tour a Victorian soup kitchen.

Then I move on to discuss the various servants, tradesmen, and professionals that might be job options for your own heroes and heroines. Plus, I'll be sharing some of the helpful advice from the period.

I'll tackle the impact of slavery and racism during the Georgian years, and highlight the changing laws and public opinions of the slave trade, before I show you ways to incorporate more ethnic diversity into your work in an authentic way.

No book with the word "harlot" in its title would skip over prostitution and sex, and I've dedicated an entire chapter to the ladies (and men!) of the night. I'll explore straight and queer prostitutes, and the public opinions on the men and women who serviced others.

After that, we'll explore hygiene and medicine, including abortion, hospitals, and germs. No book on the Victorian era would be complete without a chapter dedicated to the many technological advances leading up to and during the Industrial Revolution.

There are also two appendix sections at the back to help with terms from the period and a timeline to keep track of major events. Also, keep your eyes open for biographies on some lesser known folks from the era.

With all that out of the way, shall we get started scrubbing Mr. Darcy's chamber pots?

# Things You Need to Know

## What's a Georgian?

I'm going to throw around words like Georgian, Victorian, and Regency. I'm covering a diverse time period and there isn't one label that I can apply. This book covers Dr. Johnson's England, Georgian England, the Regency, the early, mid and late Victorian eras, Dickens's London, Jack the Ripper's London. The list goes on.

I mention specific periods by name. To avoid any confusion, these are the definitions I use:

**Georgian England**: The Georgian period covers the Georges, from 1714 to 1830, when George I, II, III, and IV reigned.

**The Regency**: The Regency period was when "Mad King George" (George III) couldn't tend to his duties due to mental illness, so his son, the Prince of Wales, ruled as a proxy under the title of Prince Regent from 1811 to 1820 (the death of his father). Many people extend this period to beyond these dates for various reasons, extending it all the way back to 1795 or thereabouts.

I typically use the term inclusive of Napoleonic wars (starting in 1803), but excluding the French revolutionary wars.

**Victorian England**: This covers the long reign of Queen Victoria, from 1837 to 1901, and saw the country's population nearly double, as well as the agricultural and industrial revolutions. For simplicity's sake, I'm also making the arbitrary decision to include King William IV (1830-1837) as a part of the "early Victorian" era in this book.

Check out the glossary at the end of the book if you're looking for more information on the various monarchs that reigned during these eras.

This book isn't written in chronological order; it is organized by topics and not dates. When making notes for your next novel, remember that there's nearly a century's gap between George III's death and Victoria's death. Just as so many things changed between WWI and today, the same thing can be said for the 19th century. It's important when writing an 1843 steampunk, let's say, to ensure that the railroad line actually connected the heroine's town with London before she hops on the train to save the day!

## Money Matters: What's a d?

I talk a lot about money in the book. Since you might not be familiar with the old currency system, here is a crash course on the financial terms I use in this book:

*d* – This means penny or pence. It's abbreviated in the period with a *d* not *p*, as in a Roman *denarius* not penny. It takes twelve pence to make a shilling.

*s* – Twelve pence made a shilling. Four shillings is written *4s*. Twenty shillings made a pound.

£ - The pound sterling is sometimes written *l* so eight pounds might be written *8l* as opposed to today's more common £8. I use £ in the book, though *l* might be used in direct quotes from the period.

There are plenty of other financial terms like halfpenny, crown, guinea, quid, and so on. These are all listed and explained in the glossary at the back of the book.

If you're having a difficult time understanding the financials and needing a modern reference, I recommend using the quick and dirty "multiply by 50" rule recommended by Venetia Murray in *An Elegant Madness* (1998). If you need a more concise comparison, there are a number of historical currency converters online that take fluctuating inflation rates into account.

None of these calculations account for the impact of technology on our lives; I have a washing machine and not a laundress. Not to mention my washing machine cost a lot more than a laundress would in Austen's time! Always use caution when updating prices to modern times.

## Jane Austen
## (1775-1817)

Jane was the daughter of a clergyman and, while never wealthy, the Austen family lived comfortably. After finishing school, she began writing seriously.

Austen lost her beloved father early in 1805. Though dependent upon her brothers, Austen's poverty was relative. Austen, her elder sister, and her mother all moved into Chawton Cottage, owned by one of Austen's brothers. Mrs. Austen brought an income of £460 per annum and Cassandra, Austen's elder sister, had a small annual sum of money, too. Austen was somewhere between comparatively comfortable and on the edge of poverty for most of her adult life.

It was at Chawton Cottage that Austen became more prolific than ever. Austen's brother, Henry, doubled as her literary agent and successfully had *Sense and Sensibility* published in 1811. *Pride and Prejudice* came out in 1813 and was a commercial success. *Mansfield Park* and *Emma* were published with financial and critical success.

Austen ignored the decline in her health in early 1816 and continued to write. She managed to finish *The Elliots* (known today as *Persuasion*) before becoming bedridden. Austen died on July 18, 1817, leaving behind a literary legacy.

# Chapter 1: How Poor is Poor?

*"He swore and he drank, he was dirty and gross."*
-Fanny Price, about her father (Jane Austen, *Mansfield Park*)

The Regency period has all of the makings of an award-winning, daytime soap opera. At the helm, we have a mentally-unstable king and his drunken, debt-ridden gambler son. There are balls, house parties, marriages, scandals, intrigues, seductions, war, and novels. No wonder people love this time period!

This is a world where the word "poverty" has very different meanings. The son of an Earl who purchases a military commission might consider his situation poor, though the common troops under his command would have a rather different perspective. The slave boy who follows behind a naval captain in London will see the world through a different filter than the family who cannot afford to buy their own carriage.

Many of us have an idealized image of the past and there is perhaps no other time more romanticized than the Regency and Victorian periods. Bustles and bonnets, boots and boudoirs. The stuff of fantasies. While I am typically a jeans-and-Tee kinda gal, every so often I want to put on a pretty dress and go to a ball. On

1

those days, I want to live in a time when men walk around in tight boots pulled over even tighter wool trousers. And I want to live in a world where I can shop for haberdashery to sew on my bonnets and dresses.

Heck, I'd settle for a world where I get to say "haberdashery" on a regular basis.

I have no problem with fantasies. It doesn't bother me all that much when the past gets romanticized. But for this book, I want to talk about all of the people missing from the movie adaptations, from the steampunk novels, and from the Regency romances: the poor people.

Consider your heroine's status in the world. A woman born into the landed gentry who has lost income will wonder which of her family and friends she should beg for assistance and her care. A woman born to working class parents will assume no one would take care of her, and would hunt for employment.

I came into this book with a good grounding in what "poor" looked like in a Georgian or Victorian setting. However, this book is for you. I wanted to know what everyone out there saw as poor. I turned to social media and posed the question, "When you think of the Regency era, who do you consider poor?"

It was a tricky question, but a writer's got to start somewhere. The Regency period is just a small period that this book intersects, but it is a trendy time period. If you know of the Regency period, it's probably because of Jane Austen. Perhaps you own all of her books, movies, modern variations, and manners guides. On the other hand, perhaps you were forced to watch *Pride and Prejudice* in 1995 by your university sweetheart and still mourn the loss of those six hours.

The examples that came back were quite interesting. Most were creations of Austen herself (and we can argue all day if Austen is Regency or Georgian, so let's skip right along), which fits very well with a book to help fiction writers. Amongst the list were:

- Charlotte Lucas (*Pride and Prejudice*) was the daughter of a businessman-turned-knight. She married a creepy weirdo so that she could have her own home and not be a spinster left to the care of her father and brothers.

- Miss Bates (*Emma*) was the unmarried daughter of a deceased clergyman, whose death left her and her elderly mother with little to live on.
- Anne Elliot (*Persuasion*): Her titled father had a shopping addiction and had spent most of their family money. He had to rent out his ancestral home and move into a cheaper apartment elsewhere.
- Tiny Tim (*A Christmas Carol*): This is Victorian, but it's a popular story all the same. Tim needed medical treatment, but Scrooge wouldn't pay Tim's father a high enough salary to afford the doctor and medicines.
- Jane Austen (1775-1817): She was unmarried and had no inherited money of her own, thus completely dependent upon her brothers and whatever money she made writing.

What's striking is that, in the case of the women in this list, none were allowed or expected to work. They had servants and relied on the charity and good-will of others. Now, having a servant or helper wasn't unusual for impoverished people of the era; this was a time before microwave ovens and laundry machines. But consider, however poor old Miss Bates might have been, the maid-of-all-work that worked for her would have been even poorer.

It's at this juncture that we must butt up against the myth that *women didn't work back then.*

Most women worked jobs, as did most men. They worked for themselves or others, but they worked nonetheless. Money didn't grow on trees. The meager social safety net that existed was appalling. The majority of British people worked bloody hard just to survive. Balls, fine muslin, and crinolines were things of fantasy for many teenaged girls, as were the horses, sports cars–

I mean *curricles*—and fine claret.

More people were poor, as opposed to comfortable. Even fewer were wealthy, and still less were rich. According to Charles Booth, 31% of late-Victorian London's residents lived in poverty. The majority of the rest just above poverty, and most had fallen into poverty at one point in their lives.

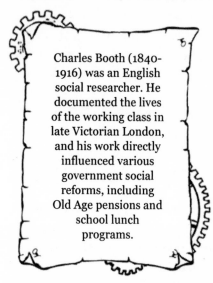

Charles Booth (1840-1916) was an English social researcher. He documented the lives of the working class in late Victorian London, and his work directly influenced various government social reforms, including Old Age pensions and school lunch programs.

Outside of actual times of famine, very few died from starvation. Hunger and malnutrition, by contrast, were rampant. Today, we'd call this *food insecurity*—not having access to reliable, healthy, affordable food on a regular basis. The working poor interviewed by researchers such as Booth lived in crowded, poorly-ventilated rooms with little means to dispose of waste. Their water supplies were unsafe, if they existed at all. Work itself was consistently inconsistent[1]. This grittier perspective is very different from the movie adaptations of flowing gowns and frivolous thoughts.

I don't fault any writer for thinking that women such as the infamous Georgiana Cavendish, Duchess of Devonshire (1757-1806), were a dime a dozen. Georgiana's life has been highlighted in several books, paintings, and even a feature film. During her lifetime, she travelled in such exalted circles that the Prince Regent himself once had a temper tantrum in her foyer.

So when writers sit down to write a poor family in Regency London, it's easy to think a woman relying on her wealthy brothers was the poorest of the poor, excluding maybe the destitute sleeping in the gutters. It's understandable to mistake that no women worked, since we don't often see heroines working in the most popular books from the era, with the exception of being a governess—and the most famous of those inherited a fortune and married a wealthy man. Ladies in more modern novels sometimes enter a romanticized version of prostitution, where everyone is a glamorous courtesan and not addicted to gin, where their first client rescues them with a marriage proposal.

I've read plenty of romances and adventure books where women living in the "depths of poverty" were well-educated, lived in three-bedroom apartments, received small annuities to keep them afloat, and travelled extensively in their own little part of the world. For a duchess, sure, that would be poverty. For most Londoners, that would be winning the life lottery.

## Introducing Mark and Martha

What is a book without characters? Throughout this book, I'll be telling stories through Martha and Mark's (fictional) lives to help put the history into context.

Martha Dudley is our Georgian heroine. Her father is a shipwright at the dockyard and her mother a seamstress, though frequent pregnancies have weakened her. Her grandfather was a child slave, but had self-emancipated himself after the Somerset ruling and worked as a footman for the rest of his life for a wealthy family. He left Martha and her eldest sister enough money in his will for a basic education. Martha's nineteen, single, and a lady's maid for a middle-class elderly woman and hopes to marry a dressmaker so that they can open a bespoke dress and drapery shop together.

Mark James is our Victorian steampunk hero, in London seeking his fortune and looking for some excitement. His father owns a successful shop in Bristol. He has a small income of his own, an annuity from his grandfather, who'd been a shop owner as well. Mark has no interest in being a shop keeper and has been well-educated, so now he's in the city to find a career better suited to his tastes. Perhaps the law, or maybe even some minor, none-life-threatening espionage. He's twenty, single, and hopes to either find a profession or, even better, a wealthy woman to support his love of cards and curricles.

Martha and Mark will experience all of the ups and downs of our story. Feel free to borrow any of these ideas and writing prompts for your stories—even their names and history are up for grab!

## Show Me the Money

I'll be tossing around salaries and costs from different years in this book. That can get confusing without some context, so let's start this section with the income brackets and where the glass ceiling exists.

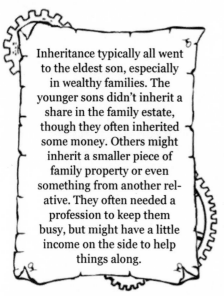

Inheritance typically all went to the eldest son, especially in wealthy families. The younger sons didn't inherit a share in the family estate, though they often inherited some money. Others might inherit a smaller piece of family property or even something from another relative. They often needed a profession to keep them busy, but might have a little income on the side to help things along.

First, Joseph Massie in 1759 decided to compile information on the average family income in England. He used recorded salaries and incomes from a statistic survey that had been recently taken. He determined that half the total population of England made an annual income of £23 or less *per household* (so this figure includes everyone's earnings). Massie puts this as the bottom rung. Basically what we'd today call the poverty line.

In London specifically, labourers were making at the time £27.10s a year, so they were just above the poverty line cut off. Skilled tradesmen and builders were in the £40 per annum range, so better.

Stories of the period sometimes lead us to believe that the

clergy were rolling in wealth, but they were only being paid £50 to £100 per year. Since a number of clergy were younger sons, they might have inherited money or a small piece of property which would supplement their income. Those without that might take up small-scale farming, private tutoring, and similar ventures available to a decently-educated fellow.

Clerks were also in the £50 range, whereas educated professionals like those in law were making in the range of £200 a year. Some very successful merchants were easily making £600 a year.

At the very top of the income graph were ten families who made an eye-stunning average of £27,000 per annum.

To put all of that in perspective, a tract in 1734 outlined the budget for a labourer, his wife, and four children living in London. The grocery bill set aside funds for meat, bread, and butter, as well as root vegetables, salt, and sugar. Small amounts of cheese and milk were budgeted. Bread and beer expenditures were about equal. Money was set aside for soap, candles, and various mending needs. Their total costs worked out to about 4d a head per day.

The labourer was bringing in between 9d and 10d a day (about £12-£13 a year), leaving precious little for housing, new clothing and shoes, and medical attention. His wife and children would need to work to help earn their share of the expenses and contribute to savings for emergencies.

A century later in 1861, a man named Dudley Baxter divided Britain's social classes by looking at their annual income. He drew the upper class dividing line at those bringing in over £1000 a year. The middle class was making in the range of £100 to £999 a year. The working class earned under £100 per year.

Baxter's classification is useful for modern readers, though it doesn't take into account class snobbery. Certain people would always be middle class . . . even if their shops made them millions.

Because.

*So there.*

Things weren't much better for the working class in Baxter's time. In 1856, the household budget for a labourer, his wife, and their four children doesn't show any great improvement in circumstances.

His salary was £1.10s per week, which is about £78 per year, assuming he had constant work. His weekly rent for two rooms—rooms!—was 4s. They spent another 5s on food and fuel, 3d on tobacco, a 9d weekly fee to a sick club, and ½d weekly for each child to spend on a treat. Their basic weekly expenditures were 11s.1d, leaving them around 19s for any transportation needs, new clothing costs and laundry, plus savings in case of illness and pregnancy[2]. The woman of the house would need to work, as would the older children, to keep them ahead and to have a buffer in case the father became ill or injured.

If your hero is a foreman at the local airship dock, he'd be concerned if one of the general labourers was seen about town dressed in fancy clothes, or even if he could afford to eat at fancier eateries every day. This is a man who should be struggling to make ends meet, as opposed to flaunting his cash. Those were the men who either had gambling habits or were stealing from the company. He might even be working for the French.

*Merde.*

## Does This Apartment Have Free Internet?

Who hasn't had sub-standard housing during their early adulthood? You know the place I'm talking about. It was so cold that the cat slept in your sleeping bag with you because you couldn't afford to turn up the heat. The hot water heater only worked if you stood on one foot and hummed.

Maybe you've had a place like a summer sublet I had in university. The building had an earwig infestation. I've always been terrified of those things, so I called the landlord in a panic. He inspected the bathroom that was crawling with them, mused how earwigs rarely made it up to the second floor of a building, and suggested I get a can of Raid and wear ear plugs until hatching season passed.

And while horrible, those apartments weren't close to the slums that existed in Georgian times, nor during the heart of the Industrial Revolution, when too many people were living in too small of a space.

When I did inner-city work, I'd hear all of the stories about condemned houses and houses that should be condemned, and I think these buildings are closer to the slums of historic London. One infamous house had a mother and her small kids living in a windowless basement room across a river of open sewage. The pipes were missing, so the upstairs toilets emptied into this river that cut across the concrete floor to the drain, with a wooden plank across it for walking.

Another building had a cracked foundation. When I say cracked, I mean I stood in the basement and could quite clearly see outdoors. And put my hand through the hole to pick some grass. With temperatures regularly dropping to -30C, this was obviously not a safe place to live.

These rundown firetraps are closer to the types of houses your very poor heroes are going to rent. With a bit more money, better housing will come: just like today.

For someone like Mark, he'd easily spend 2s to 3s a week just to rent a room! Not an apartment or a house, but a single room. If you are writing about a family, they might rent two rooms, which could run around the 4s a week in the mid-eighteenth-century. These rooms didn't typically have ranges, private bathrooms, running water en suite, and all of those luxuries, though they did improve as services became more widely available.

Not everyone lived in complete squalor. Martha's father was a shipwright, so he was a tradesman. Her mother was a seamstress when she was well enough to sew, and all of the children worked. Martha and two of her sisters lived elsewhere, helping to reduce family expenses further, plus providing the girls the opportunity to save for emergencies and to send money home if needed.

Mid-income working folks in 1815 were able to rent an entire house, as opposed to just a room. These were narrow houses with three or four stories. Each floor was a different room, such as the bedrooms or the kitchen, but they gave a family a bit of room to live and eat.

Better houses were built in 1841 to help accommodate the growing middle income of the working class. These houses were in the range of 3s.6d per week. They were pricier than the more common rental spaces, but the increased rent brought a number of benefits. The buildings came with water access, communal laundry, and a place to dry clothes. A house like this could provide a woman and her daughters with additional income, as she could take on small amounts of laundry and ironing every week.

Some of these improved houses even had a small patch of garden (key to growing a few herbs and pea plants) and were in the 5s per week price range[3].

Still, can you imagine how crowded Martha's house would have been? Children and teens coming and going, rushing about to get to their various jobs and schools. Servants and helpers in and out of the house doing their jobs. Mrs. Dudley trying to finish her sewing while yelling at the nursemaid to get the toddlers away from her before they spilled something. It would have been anything but calm and tranquil.

I recently read a series of Regency romances that had the poor heroine reduced to common street prostitution to pay for her several-room apartment and two servants. Poor thing sold her virginity on the street for only £1, which you'll see later how much of a bargain price this was for London.

A lot of things stood out in this scenario, but perhaps the biggest was that she had running water on demand 24/7 directly into her apartment and it seemed to never suffer from water pressure issues. And it never stank.

London did benefit from new technologies before smaller towns and the countryside and piped in water was one such benefit. However, don't assume your own heroines will have ready access to water.

The water supply was privately owned and operated.

Residents might get water, of dubious quality, for an hour three times a week. If you missed when the pipes were coming on, oh well, so make sure your heroine stocks up. Don't be surprised if poor Mrs. Dudley has a few buckets of water in the corner of her kitchen[4].

The homeless always seek out the warmest, safest places they can find in the winter months. Where did your heroine sleep when she was homeless two years ago? Did she just cuddle up with a blanket on the street? That would be risky because she could be picked up for vagrancy, or perhaps even worse, someone might steal her boots and blanket while she slept.

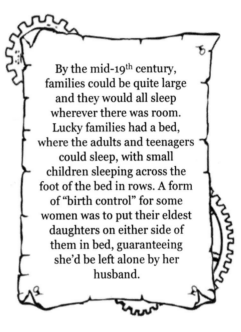

By the mid-19th century, families could be quite large and they would all sleep wherever there was room. Lucky families had a bed, where the adults and teenagers could sleep, with small children sleeping across the foot of the bed in rows. A form of "birth control" for some women was to put their eldest daughters on either side of them in bed, guaranteeing she'd be left alone by her husband.

If you want to add a little intrigue to her backstory, but have it still be believable, she might risk the grievous crime of break and entry to spend the night in a brick kiln or glass factory. Those buildings had massive furnaces that burned all day long and continued to put out heat long after the fires had died down and the staff gone home.

Likewise, desperate homeless individuals could break into the deserted buildings for cold, but sheltered, winter accommodations. I smell a forbidden romance!

Whatever room or house your hero ends up renting, double check that it's in line with his income and location. If necessary, lock yourself up in your bathroom for a few days with your gassy dog, meat pies, and no showers to get a "you were there" smell experience. Though, I recommend not inviting your new love interest over during this experiment; the interest might fade away rather quickly.

## Please, Sir, I Want Some More

Even if you've never read Dickens in your life (I envy you), you probably will recognize the famous phrase, "Please, sir, I want some more." Oliver Twist, the orphan inmate of the dreaded workhouse, was young and hungry and had the nerve to go back and ask for more gruel.

Workhouses have never had a good image. They probably never will, as modern eyes look at them through the life of Oliver Twist, a wretched young thing who wanted nothing more than a bit more watery oatmeal. Not all workhouses were horrible, and they did improve in the later 19th century. However, there were plenty of bad ones and plenty of horror stories. People wanted to avoid them at all costs, but sometimes they were better than starving on the streets in winter.

Workhouses existed long before Oliver Twist's time. Henry Fielding (1707-1754), over a century earlier than Charles Dickens's classic tale, wrote that welfare and social assistance shouldn't be attractive. In his mind, everyone would stop working and just live off charity. He divided the poor into three groups, a categorization that modern readers will probably recognize:

- Physically unable to work.
- Able and willing to work.
- Able, but not willing to work.

Fielding believed very few people met the qualifications for physically unable to work. Those that did should be looked after by private charity. Those unwilling to work should all be imprisoned; laziness was practically criminal in his eyes. But that middle category was the problem. These were people who would work, but had no work available to them for various reasons. It turned people into beggars and vagrants, instead of hard-working members of society.

The concept of the workhouse was to keep the poor off the streets, provide impoverished children a minimal education, and give able-bodied adults something to do. Unfortunately, workhouses had little effect on poverty. In some ways, workhouses made local work shortages worse because they undercut the price of materials made and sold.

The buildings could be terrible places to live. Places like Clerkenwell workhouse held 320 inmates in the 1750s, but was built for only 150 people[5].

Workhouse inmates had to follow the long list of rules concerning things like sobriety, smoking, visitors, and general behaviour. They had curfews, routines, and an overall lifestyle that resembled prison. Things became even worse with the 1834 Poor Law Amendment Act, which made workhouses the feared, draconian, unsafe places we recognize today.

Workhouse inmates were filed under various labels, including:

- Aged and infirm men and women
- Able-bodied men and boys over thirteen
- Children above seven years of age, but under thirteen
- Children under seven years of age
- Able-bodied women and girls above sixteen

This could affect the meal portions they received, housing options within the facility, and work opportunities.

By the mid-Victorian times, there were growing reports of the abuses happening within and just outside of the workhouse doors. Reports of people in need being turned away surfaced, such as poor women in active labour and men injured in industrial accidents. Sometimes children were taken in without their parents, or the just the wife and the children. It wasn't until 1847 that married couples in their sixties could request a shared bedroom, and few facilities granted the request[6].

There was a significant amount of social shame attached to the workhouse. If Mark was reduced to living at the workhouse, anyone on the street would recognize him as such. Workhouses had uniforms that would make him easily recognizable as an inmate by the general public. This would make getting work and assistance even harder because he could labelled as just another lazy man if he wasn't visibly infirmed in some manner[7].

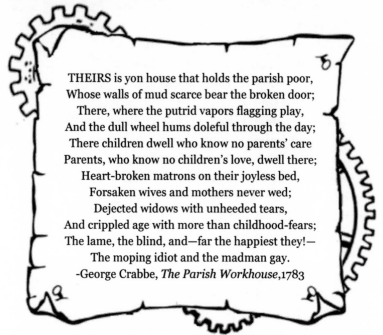

THEIRS is yon house that holds the parish poor,
Whose walls of mud scarce bear the broken door;
There, where the putrid vapors flagging play,
And the dull wheel hums doleful through the day;
There children dwell who know no parents' care
Parents, who know no children's love, dwell there;
Heart-broken matrons on their joyless bed,
Forsaken wives and mothers never wed;
Dejected widows with unheeded tears,
And crippled age with more than childhood-fears;
The lame, the blind, and—far the happiest they!—
The moping idiot and the madman gay.
-George Crabbe, *The Parish Workhouse*,1783

Your hero would do everything he could to avoid the workhouse. However, if he has a family and a sick wife, he might need to swallow his pride. Moving them into the workhouse while he worked to earn some savings might be the only thing he could do. Likewise, an ill single mother without the means to care for herself and her infant might at least have the opportunity to recover from child birth and illness long enough to get back on her feet.

## Mary Lacy 1740 – after 1773

Mary was born in 1740 and, at 19, got fed up with servant life and ran away to the sea the way any proper woman should. She called herself William Chandler and joined a ship as a carpenter's servant. She eventually got her shipwright's certificate in 1770, but ended up with rheumatism and received a pension of £20, which she claimed in her own name. She then wrote a book called *The*

*history of the female shipwright: Mary Lacy.* In her book, she revealed how concealment was carried out: getting a few trustworthy, sober, older guys to cover for you.

But, the most interesting thing (I think) is that Mary was in fact a ladies' man. She flirted with the ladies and loved every moment of it. While it was innocent, according to her memoir, looking at it now with a modern eye, I see a woman who found a way to be herself[1].

# Chapter 2: Ladies and Children First

*"Oh! My sweetest Lizzy! How rich and how great you will be! What pin-money, what jewels, what carriages you will have!"*
-Mrs. Bennet upon the engagement of her daughter, Elizabeth, to Mr. Darcy
(Jane Austen, *Pride and Prejudice*)

Women hold an interesting place in Georgian and Victorian England. Women were the keepers of morality, yet were the frequent victims of harassment and abuse. Society wouldn't have managed if it weren't for the work of women, yet they were barred from any well-paying job until the close of the 19th century and into the 20th century. They were the pillars of the home, yet given very few tools to help them achieve those expectations.

Being a woman was only great for those with ready cash and social status.

Most children didn't have long childhoods. We talk about how children today are growing up so fast. A Georgian or a Victorian would mock today's children and teenagers. A fourteen-year-old asking for an allowance? Goodness. What's next? Expecting children to not earn their keep?

This chapter is about the everyday realities of working-class and impoverished women, plus the children who worked either to support their parents and siblings, or themselves because they were on their own.

## The Female Breadwinner

One of the things that surprised me the most while researching for this book was just how many households were headed by women. I knew that there were plenty of female-led households, since many women were widowed. But I had no idea that 19% of households in the mid-1800s were led by women! And that figure excludes people living on their own.

The majority of those households were widowed women, but a fifth—*a full 20%*—were married women without their spouses living with them. These men weren't present because of a variety of reasons, including imprisonment, employment elsewhere, and abandonment. After all, just because divorce was nigh impossible doesn't mean a man was forced to stick around. If the highest of the high ranks can have a "matrimonial *fracas*," as Austen called it, certainly the lowest ranks wouldn't have any trouble with separation.

Many more households existed that relied solely on the women of the house to be the major breadwinners. The contribution of women is difficult to measure because it was widely unreported, even during a major census.

Men were the head of the house and it was left to them to fill out the census with the clerk at their door. Some men weren't aware of how much their wives financially contributed. Others were embarrassed that they relied so much on their wives' earnings, so left off her work. Still others left off the women all together, while others put the wife's occupation as the same as her husband's and just combined the incomes. All illegal work was left off the census, such as prostitution, begging, and theft[2], even if that was how a household stayed afloat.

This was a time when men's pride was tied to being able to provide for their family. Being injured or out of work was a major blow to a man's social identity. He didn't want to be seen as lazy, living off his womenfolk.

Drunkard husbands often didn't notice that their wives worked. They were too busy focusing on spending their coins getting drunk to care where the money came from. It was left to the woman of the house to work enough to feed herself and her children.

Households that relied on a woman's income pretty much guaranteed that they'd be living in poverty. Women earned significantly less than men and were more likely to work temporary, seasonal, or unstable work[3]. Once sunk into poverty, it was very difficult, if not impossible, to pull oneself back out of the abyss.

## Handy at Home

In the next chapters, we'll be talking about domestic servants. A common misconception about servants is that they all got room and board included as part of their job. For many, especially in wealthier homes, that was absolutely true. But not every household could afford to house and feed a servant. Households making only £30 a year still needed help, but they certainly couldn't afford to let someone move into their home. That's where casual work comes into play.

Let's say that Martha's father, Mr. Dudley, is injured at work. There was no short-term medical disability in this era, and the unions had not yet organized sick pools for employees. Mrs. Dudley, Martha, and all of her siblings would be relied on to bring in funds.

One of Martha's sisters, a twelve-year-old girl, looked after a neighbour's twin toddlers while their mother worked. It only paid a couple of pennies, but it was enough to pay for the girl's share in the household expenses.

Martha spoke to her mistress about the dreadful state her family was suffering under. A family friend ran a small mechanical clock shop, and the regular girl who came to clean the shop floor had been ill. So another Dudley sister was sent to the clerk office to fill in. Many small, independent offices and shops might bring in a cleaner, especially if they had no daughter of their own. It might just be a couple times a week, or a few hours a day, and it would be manual labour—wipe down the furniture, clean the coal stove, scour the floors, and scrub the outside steps and windows—but it could help a ten-year-old girl contribute to her family.

But it wasn't only the older kids who could be put to work in the most desperate of circumstances.

## Babies Make Great Employees

What was your first paying job? Lemonade entrepreneur at age ten? Paper route at age twelve? Cutting grass at age fifteen?

Mine was picking strawberries at fourteen. I'd be hunched over all day in the fields. I had to be fashionable (a boy might see me), and since it was the late 80s, baseball caps were out. My teased and hair-sprayed pony tail was propped up on one side of my head and I wore a bathing suit under my sweatpants (I needed something to protect my legs from the bugs). Back then, you lathered yourself up with baby oil so you'd burn faster. So, I got a second-degree burn on my back.

Ah, yes, the first job.

But no matter how early we started working, I doubt any of us started working at *birth*. Daycare, then as now, was expensive. One Victorian mother, for example, earned 6s.3d per week making paper bags at home. It's difficult to do anything with a baby around, so she paid 4s.6d for a nurse to look after the little one. That means *nearly three-quarters* of her income went to childcare, and unfortunately it didn't even help protect her infant. The nurse got drunk, as was often the case, and the baby died[4].

For a heroine who couldn't afford a nurse, or perhaps a poor widower left with a newborn babe and not ready to drop the wee thing off at a local church, they could rent out the baby for a small fee.

That's right: rent out the baby. Daycare wasn't used by the landed wealthy, who didn't need it, but rather by working women who couldn't earn a living and look after a baby. Daycare was expensive. A poor newborn could be rented out at a cost of 4d a day for beggars to use as props.

A young, sickly woman with a babe in her arms could easily bring in 6d or 7d a day begging in Victorian London, which meant she would clear more than a shilling a week. That would cover most of her rent in a slum, along with a little food and sundries. Plus, the mother of the infant would get her baby out of her hair for part of the day; more so if the renter was able to breastfeed.

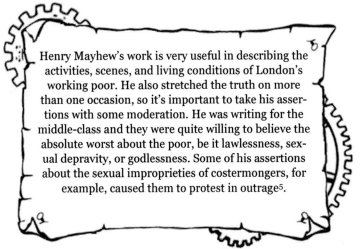

Henry Mayhew's work is very useful in describing the activities, scenes, and living conditions of London's working poor. He also stretched the truth on more than one occasion, so it's important to take his assertions with some moderation. He was writing for the middle-class and they were quite willing to believe the absolute worst about the poor, be it lawlessness, sexual depravity, or godlessness. Some of his assertions about the sexual improprieties of costermongers, for example, caused them to protest in outrage[5].

Can you imagine if Mark got some poor, young woman pregnant? He couldn't marry her, since his middle-class family would never approve of him bringing home a beggar. He decides to visit the baby, and drop off some food, linens, and the like, only to discover she's been rented out as a prop near the theatres. Would he be angry that his lover rented out his baby, pleased by her financial shrewdness, or be shamed about not having provided either of them enough money to survive?

The penny wages earned by children could mean the difference between solvency and the dreaded workhouse. Henry Mayhew was a social reformer in the mid-Victorian era and wrote extensively on London's poor. He highlights the life of a nameless costergirl, aged seven, and a costerboy, aged sixteen.

The costergirl started her day at four in the morning. With some money supplied by her parents, she purchased a bulk amount of whatever was seasonable and affordable, be it oranges, apples, violets, or watercress. She walked all day, selling her wares in smaller, more individual sized amounts, until nine at night. She might earn 1s.6d that day, which she'd use to purchase a pound of bread to eat during the day and help pay for supplies the next day. Her net earnings were only a few pennies by the end of the day, but it was enough to keep her parents out of the poorhouse.

The boy was fatherless and grew up with his mother and his siblings. When he was little, his mother worked from six in the morning to ten at night. He'd have to beg in the streets if he got hungry while his mother was at work. Eventually, he was old enough to get a job earning 4d a morning; the job included breakfast. He saved money and later went into business with his brother, allowing their mother to stay at home and cook, plus do odd job jobs. They made 2s.6d a day by selling greens in the morning and nuts outside of public buildings at night[6].

There were plenty of odd jobs that were perfectly suited for children and young teenagers. A few summers ago, I hired all of the teenagers on my street to clean up my backyard, including trimming branches, shifting my giant composter, and picking apples. The same existed in Georgian and Victorian times.

In the mid-Victorian, a ten-year-old girl made 1s 6d a week working six twelve-hour days as a maid. The master of the house would spend the same amount on a pair of silk hose.

A widow, or abandoned woman, with no adult male in the house could survive if she had several sons in their teens. Boys were paid more than girls, so a couple of sons could help keep their mother out of the workhouse. A twelve-year-old boy could chop firewood and load crates on wagons; in the 1750s, he could make 1½d per hour doing that. If a boy chopped wood for the morning, he'd earn enough to buy a pound of cheese, plus some low-grade coal and a few candles for home.

Boys could run errands for gentlemen and hold horses for them, ensuring they weren't stolen in the questionable parts of the city. They might only be paid ¼d, but those added up quickly over the span of a day.

Even though girls weren't paid as much as boys, they were still useful. There was plenty of work available for girls, and their earnings were often enough to pay their portion of their room and board at home. A six-year-old girl could help entertain the neighbour's toddler for the price of a hot meal. That meal might save Mom and Dad a ½d and it also gave the toddler's mother an opportunity to do one of the many at-home jobs available to her.

Girls were often hired as "Saturday Girls" to work on Saturdays to scrub the front steps of homes. Mayhew tells of an eight-year-old girl who was hired to help a Jewish middle-class family. They let her sleep over Friday night, so that she could tend their fires and snuff out candles on the Sabbath. They fed her very well. At home, she only ate bread, butter, and some-

> The great detective, Sherlock Holmes, used a rabble of "dirty and ragged little street-Arabs" for his unofficial information and errand force, the Baker Street Irregulars. Led by Wiggins (BBC Sherlock fans will also recognize the name), the homeless children were paid a shilling to assist Sherlock, and paid upwards of a guinea for vital clues.

times tea. The Jewish family fed her "a reg'lar good lot to eat," with a supper on Friday night, fried fish on Saturday morning, meat for dinner, and sometimes meat for supper later Saturday night. They even gave her toys, the only ones she owned.

Obviously, not everyone was as nice as that family, but perhaps your heroine's middle class family might take their responsibilities as employers very seriously.

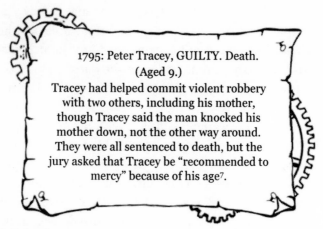

1795: Peter Tracey, GUILTY. Death.
(Aged 9.)
Tracey had helped commit violent robbery
with two others, including his mother,
though Tracey said the man knocked his
mother down, not the other way around.
They were all sentenced to death, but the
jury asked that Tracey be "recommended to
mercy" because of his age[7].

# Child Labour

The jobs available to children in the Georgian and Victorian eras are staggering. Many were benign, easy jobs, such as running errands for the master of the house. Others were long and monotonous, such as selling flowers to passing gentlemen. But then some jobs were dangerous, life-shortening, disabling jobs.

Parishes apprenticed out their orphans once they were around nine years of age; in the 18th century, some were put out as early as seven. Children didn't get a say in where they were sent and risked beatings, malnutrition, exposure, and death.

Children were bound as apprentices until they were adults. Boys were bound until they were twenty-four, and girls until twenty-one. Girls had the benefit of being rescued by marriage, though that brought with it a new set of risks.

Running away wasn't much of an option, though many did. It was illegal to run away, and run-away apprentices were treated little better than run-away slaves. Notices were put in the papers and it was difficult to find work after that.

A law passed in 1767 limited the apprenticeship period to no more than seven years, but this did not stop the dead-end nature of the system. It was designed to train children in a skill, to give them a means to supporting themselves financially as adults.

Unfortunately, too many masters took the £2 to £3 paid to them for taking on a children and didn't actually teach the kids anything. Many of the children were left to do the menial tasks the master didn't want to do, as opposed to learning the skill of milliner, draper, and so on.

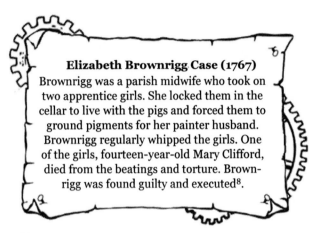

**Elizabeth Brownrigg Case (1767)**
Brownrigg was a parish midwife who took on two apprentice girls. She locked them in the cellar to live with the pigs and forced them to ground pigments for her painter husband. Brownrigg regularly whipped the girls. One of the girls, fourteen-year-old Mary Clifford, died from the beatings and torture. Brownrigg was found guilty and executed[8].

## Education

The two hundred years between the 1700s to the dawn of the Edwardian age saw huge changes in the education of the masses. Learning was important; everyone knew it. However, education was a privilege and not a right for a very long time.

The wealthy were educated at home by a governess, private tutors, or possibly by the parents. If no governess was hired, girls were educated by their mothers, supplemented with whatever reading material their fathers or the local lending library could offer them. Wealthy boys were sent to boarding schools and many later went to university.

The working class had limited access to charity schools, Sunday schools, and various volunteer efforts. Most schools were for boys. In 1766, for example, the Merchant Taylors' school charged a sliding scale fee. Some kids paid nothing, others paid 2s to 4d a week. They learned Latin, Greek, and Hebrew, and a bit of the social graces. Other schools focused on math, reading, writing, and book-keeping.

A poor girl's education wasn't much to talk about. Well-to-do girls were learning mathematics, dancing, singing, French, Italian, history, various musical instruments, drawing, and sewing and embroidery. Their working class counterparts, if lucky, were learning basic sewing skills, basic math, basic literacy, and how to do chores. Some learned useful, money-earning skills, though, such as lace-making, straw-plaiting, and knitting. These weren't high-paying jobs, but they were skills that would allow income supplementation later in life.

One of the most infamous girl's schools in literature was Lowood School for Girls in Charlotte Brontë's *Jane Eyre.* Lowood was based on Cowan Bridge School, a charity school that was attended by the Brontë sisters. They were fed burnt porridge and made to wash in freezing water; the image of the girls bashing the ice from their wash bins was real.

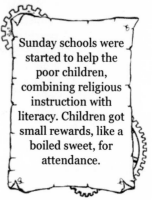

Sunday schools were started to help the poor children, combining religious instruction with literacy. Children got small rewards, like a boiled sweet, for attendance.

Girls weren't taught the heavy "male" subjects as teenage girls until the 1860s because of a fear that menstruation exhausted a girl's strength and energy. Making her learn would just make things even worse, and who knows what monster she'd turn into as an adult.

These hysterics were only focused on wealthy women. Poor girls were learning skills and working manual labour all of their lives. No one cared if the girls were on their periods; the work had to be done[9].

Charity and for-fee "public" schools began to evolve in the early years of the 1800s to a style of classroom many of us recognize today. The one teacher-many grades style began to develop. Later, several different school boards developed to cater to different types of students. Teachers and school monitors (many were children and teens themselves) with yard sticks beat misbehaving children. Dunce caps were commonplace. Religious instruction varied, from the occasional mention of the Christian Bible, to hellfire and brimstone sermons about damnation.

The very poor were unable to afford these schools. Any children in the workhouse system were left to learn there, but the system was notoriously bad. An inspection was done in 1868. They found one workhouse school being run by a thirteen-year-old girl. Another school didn't have any students who could read. Still another school had hired two illiterate teachers who had held their positions for years because they kept their students quiet.

Workhouse schools were discovered to be violent, going far beyond the corporal punishment of a strap across the knuckles. Children were brutally flogged for the smallest errors.

It wasn't until the 1880s that school was finally compulsory for children between the age of five and ten. Education became free in the state-run schools by 1891.

## Making Ends Meet

How did these families in poverty make ends meet? Sadly, the impact of poverty usually fell on women. Any shortfall in household budgets was often the woman's issue to deal with. When food was scarce, she went hungry. Since a beating could often be a fact of life for these women, she'd rather go without than face her drunkard husband's wrath for having less food on his plate.

Women obtained credit and tried to find ways to pay it back. Or simply never paid their bills. They didn't replace their clothes, relying on mending until the clothes were reduced to thin rags. Pawning everything they owned was always an option for quick money. If they

Francis Otter stole three loaves of bread from a baker's basket, worth 2d in 1746. She was found guilty, but considered a "poor creature" and transported to America for fourteen years.[10]

didn't own anything, the children could be sent out to steal things to pawn.

If the rent was behind and there was no way to pay it, they could flee in the middle of the night and move elsewhere in the city.

Without safe, accessible, and socially-acceptable means of birth control, women were often pregnant several times in their lives. And while sex is considered a part of married life, not all women had the choice in whether or not to engage in relations. Her body was her husband's property. It wasn't even until the 20th century that countries began legally recognizing a husband could rape his own wife.

Because pregnancy wasn't dangerous enough all by itself, malnutrition also contributed to even more medical problems during pregnancy.

Maternity costs were around one guinea[11], unless she was so poor as to use a poor hospital, so women would work as close to their delivery dates as possible. Though, single women generally lost their jobs when they began to show. Isolated single or unsupported women relied on home-based tasks, such as needlework, laundry, and casual prostitution as new mothers. Without friends and family, these women would end up in the workhouse or worse.

That's not to say all of these women were left abandoned. Plenty of men did support their girlfriends throughout their pregnancies and many even went on to marry them[12]. Will the hero of your story give up gambling to support his pregnant girlfriend, or will he turn his back on her, call her an ungrateful whore, saying it was her own fault?

When Mark and other heroes like him are in the slums, away from the assassins sent to take him down because he overheard French war plans, have him take a good look around. Your hero might have never worked a day in his life, yet here he is surrounded by women and children working hard. Will it open his eyes to another world, or will he dismiss them all as vagrants and the great unwashed, well beneath his notice?

How will your Regency-era disgraced governess maintain her

three-room, middle-class house in a respectable neighbourhood, when she doesn't have a penny to her name? A little ingenuity could fix many an error and provide an even better story!

## Um, Why Are You Touching Me?

It probably comes as no surprise that female servants faced sexual harassment and even sexual violence. A prolific diarist named Samuel Pepys, who lived a bit earlier than the period covered in this book (he died in 1703), openly wrote about fondling his maidservant's breasts every morning when she helped dress him[13].

He wasn't the only man who wrote about passing liberties taken with the female staff. In fact, Dr. Amanda Vickery has stated a few times that it shocked her how much men wrote in their diaries about having sex with their maids[14]!

Most people assume that the harassment always came from the master of the home. That did happen in many houses, but female servants also had to dodge male children and various relatives, houseguests, and even men-servants employed at the house! Mrs. Radcliffe in *A Modern System of Domestic Cookery* (1839) issues a warning to young women:

> If you live in a considerable family, where there are many men-servants, you must be very circumspect in your behavior to them. As they have in general little to do, they are for the most part saucy and pert where they dare, and are apt to take liberties on the least encouragement.

That's right, ladies. If you are the least bit polite to a man, whatever happens is your own fault. However, if you don't smile, the guys might follow you around all day telling you to smile. So you'll smile at him, and then you're leading him on. And whatever happens to you is your own fault. Sadly, not much has changed in that aspect.

The country girl seduced by her socially superior master was a part of embellished charity appeals, but affairs (both consensual and non-consensual ones) were more likely to take place between people of the same social standing and comparable backgrounds[15]. It was still a dangerous situation, since pregnancy often resulted in dismissal if found out.

Women weren't the only ones to face sexual harassment. A sixteen-year-old named Frederick Samuel Lea fended off three separate unwanted advances from men at his place of employment in 1840. Unsure of what to do, he confided in a female servant. He then told a policeman his situation, who advised him to take it up with his employer. The employer told the boy to take it up with his father. Basically, no one wanted to deal with a higher-class, wealthy man bothering a poor, young boy.

Besides, exchanging money for sex was a temptation for many young men in the lower classes, regardless of their own personal inclinations and orientations. Money was money. Eventually, George Lowndes was identified as the man harassing Lea and was sent to prison[16].

But there's another side to household politics that isn't always considered. Maid servants often defended their mistresses against violent husbands and some were even called upon to testify in courts of law. Some wives slept with their maids for protection from their husbands. There is one story of a maid hearing a sound upstairs. She came running and found the husband attacking his wife with a sword! The maid grabbed her master and managed to get him away from his wife so that she could escape and call for the man servants[17].

It was hard to be the 99% in this era, though even more so for children and women. So much responsibility was placed on their shoulders for so little return. Children didn't get childhoods, birthday parties, and Christmas Day. They got hard work, beatings, and illness. Women didn't get Girls Night Out or TGIF. They dealt with the constant threat of assault, pregnancy, and job loss, all the while trying to feed themselves and children.

## Isabella Beeton (1836-1865)

is one of the most celebrated cookbook authors and the original "domestic goddess."

Beeton was married to publisher Samuel Beeton and wrote cooking and household tips for his many publications. Many sections of her book were pulled from other sources, but she didn't refer to herself as an author, but as an editor.

At only 21, she published *The Book of Household Management* in 1861 and it was a commercial success. It sold 60,000 copies in the first year, and two million copies  by 1868. Her commentary on servants, household management, and cooking are still used as primary sources today.

Beeton died in 1865 from an infection during childbirth. But her husband wanted to keep up the idea that she lived on, since her name was a large source of income. Spin-offs and abridged versions were all published to keep up the image that a matronly Mrs. Beeton was still out there somewhere.

# Chapter 3: What's for Supper?

*"It will be perceived that I have omitted all kinds of spice except in those dishes which are intended expressly for them, as I consider they only flatter the appetite and irritate the stomach, and make it crave for more food; my object being not to create an appetite but to satisfy; and when those dishes in which spice is introduced are given to the poor, it should only be done by the advice of a medical man."*
– Alexis Soyer, *Soyer's Charitable Cookery (1847)*

It's difficult to say exactly what London's poor ate. There is no one go-to meal that I can point to and say, "they ate that." However, through the novels of Charles Dickens, Henry Fielding, and Jane Austen, as well as the prolific social work of people like Henry Mayhew and William Booth, we can make some accurate deductions.

One of the largest obstacles in pointing out a "typical" meal for the poor is that the poor were a varied bunch of folk. Some worked as domestics and lived with their employers. Those individuals had their meals included as a part of their compensation; getting a good position in a grand house would be a boon for anyone.

The lowly members of the navy and army were poor in terms of earnings, especially when first starting out, but they did get rations as a part of their allotment. There was also the opportunity for war prizes. War prizes didn't always come in the form of French gold, but in crates of citrus fruits and potatoes.

Since a large portion of the poor lived at home and worked there or nearby, let's start by looking at their plates. First, recall that many of these very poor rooms didn't have proper chimneys, ranges, and so on until into the Victorian era. Some houses did have shared cooking facilities, where tenants might have had an hour to cook a Sunday meal. Others might have had the facilities in their rooms, but occupants couldn't afford the coal or the time to cook during the work week.[1]

In Mark's quest to find an exciting job where he doesn't actually have to work, he gets hired as an informant posing as a clerk at one of the shipyards. There's a rumour a spy is stealing the plans for Britain's top secret steam-powered battleship and it's Mark's job to flush out the spy. They're paying him well for it, too. He gets his clerk's salary of £100 per year and the promise of £50 if he helps catch the traitor.

Before cast iron ranges were invented, cooking was done over open fire. Wood was an early fuel source. Fireplaces would be made of brick or stone, a chimney, and a wrought iron grate. This provided a place for meat to roast, plus space for a kettle and a pot.

Coal replaced wood as a fuel source in the cities, so the cooking grates were raised and widened to accommodate the small coal pieces and the hotter fire it produced. Meat was roasted in front of a fire, not over it, since coal smoke didn't improve flavour. This open system was eventually replaced with the closed cast iron range.

Mark pretends to be a low man on the ladder at work by moving into a single room at a local boarding house. His room has a small coal fireplace with an old-style cooking insert installed in the fireplace. It was small, but good enough for him to heat his room, boil a kettle, and bake a meat pie. But who has time to cook up meat pies when there are spies to catch and women to flirt with? Someone like Mark would rely heavily on grab-and-go vendor food.

Fast food sounds so modern, but the concept is quite ancient. Ready-made food was everywhere. The market districts were full of food vendors, many of the entrepreneurs getting up well before dawn to purchase and prepare their wares for the daily march of morning workers.

Mayhew lists out a costermonger's eating habits for a day and it's as grab-and-go as any modern hectic day. He said they spent a penny or so on breakfast at a coffee-stall, usually picking up coffee and two "thin"–two thin slices of buttered bread. Dinner was rarely eaten at home, with the costermonger picking up "block ornaments." That was slang for the small, dark pieces of meat that had been exposed on a butcher's block all day. They could pick up a half of pound for 2d and have it cooked in a tap-room or chophouse.

Someone who still had more selling to do that night would grab a hot pie or two. Mayhew notes that fruit pies, when in season, were very popular. I can see why. After eating nothing but salted, pickled, and dried meat and fish for months and months, fruit in any form would be a welcomed treat. Plus, you can never go wrong with pie.

On weekends, the costermongers often could afford a joint of meat at home, with a half of a shoulder being a popular and inexpensive choice. They often also picked up, or made, baked potatoes with it.

But was that enough to live off?

## How Much Did They Need?

We modern folk are generally trying to reduce the amount of food we eat, whereas our working Georgian and Victorian contemporaries were constantly looking for more. It's estimated that men and women spent 55-70 hours per week doing physical activity.

After writing that, I've now relocated myself to the treadmill desk to continue writing this book. I have to catch up to those Victorians somehow.

With that much activity, men and women would need anywhere from 2500-4500 calories every day! So, what does that look like? Well, 3000 calories is 12 slices of Safeway-brand whole wheat bread, 5 ounces of cheese, 2 large onions, 6 carrots and about 7 ounces of beef. That's a lot of food, especially on a tight budget and no electric range.

## Breaking One's Fast

Breakfast was the first meal of the day for anyone who could afford it. It might be as simple as some toast (or a bun) with tea or coffee, with poorer folks having small beer.

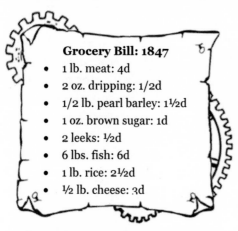

**Grocery Bill: 1847**
- 1 lb. meat: 4d
- 2 oz. dripping: 1/2d
- 1/2 lb. pearl barley: 1½d
- 1 oz. brown sugar: 1d
- 2 leeks: ½d
- 6 lbs. fish: 6d
- 1 lb. rice: 2½d
- ½ lb. cheese: 3d

Today, we typically are urged to eat breakfast as soon as we rise in the morning. Rising times varied through the eras, depending upon the family and their schedules. Factory workers might begin as early as seven in the morning. Agricultural workers were up at dawn.

Many people did not get the opportunity to eat breakfast as soon as they woke and had to work several hours before they had time for anything to eat. This would be especially true for anyone in domestic service, unless they held a position that didn't include housing and lived at home. They could eat at home, or on their way to work.

Of course, if someone was really hungry, she could always sneak a crust of bread when no one was looking.

For example, the Dudley's had a decent home, with a small, cast iron stove. Mrs. Dudley was ill and the maid hadn't arrived yet, so there was no hot breakfast available. Martha's sister, Sally, has a short-term position so she can't wait for breakfast. She could still pick up something hot from over three hundred food vendors that cropped up in manufacturing districts.

She'd have her choice of a mug of coffee, tea, or chocolate, drinking from the provided cup before handing it back. Her hot drink would have cost her about a penny or so. It wasn't a huge cost for her, but for many of the poor, the penny was far cheaper than the cost of renting a house with kitchen privileges or the cost of coal, gas, and the other fuels that came later in the century.

After knocking back her caffeinated beverage of choice on a bitter January morning, she could pick up a slice of what we'd today call coffee cake for another halfpenny and maybe a boiled egg for another penny or so. During the winter, picking up a hot potato for a halfpenny would have sure hit the spot first thing in the morning, too.

It was common for the working class to eat on the go during the work week. Food was about survival and not about social gatherings. These fast food kiosks were for the working class, offering "cheap

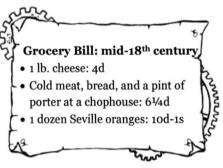

**Grocery Bill: mid-18<sup>th</sup> century**
- 1 lb. cheese: 4d
- Cold meat, bread, and a pint of porter at a chophouse: 6¼d
- 1 dozen Seville oranges: 10d-1s

meals of amazing variety that catered to tired, hurried people who could not see too much cooking themselves[2]." Basically, it's like any modern event where a hundred food trucks park outside, only this version is with wooden carts and stalls.

Many poorer folks had "small beer" with breakfast, which is similar to a lite or even as low as a dealcoholized beer (depending upon the recipe and distilling methods). Most sources put the alcohol content somewhere between 2-3.5%. In case you're not a beer drinker, a Guinness Original is 5% here in Canada, whereas a Sleeman Light is 4%.

Even children drank beer or milk; they never drank water. Today, it's difficult for us to imagine giving beer or ale to a child. However, the water was practically poisonous and the beer had vital nutrients in it to help a growing child who wouldn't have access to them through food.

## Luncheon for the Professional

The mid-meal lunch, or luncheon, was an evolving meal. In Georgian times, lunch didn't really exist as a formal meal. If a person rose very early and had breakfast, they might grab a snack mid-day, especially if they worked manual labour. Even then, shops and vendors sold pies, pastries, and ready-to-eat items like oysters, bread, cheese, and so on.

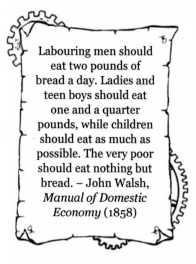

Labouring men should eat two pounds of bread a day. Ladies and teen boys should eat one and a quarter pounds, while children should eat as much as possible. The very poor should eat nothing but bread. – John Walsh, *Manual of Domestic Economy* (1858)

As the industrial revolution took hold, more and more people were working in the city full-time. With long work hours and no chance to go home for a break, lunch developed and is quickly recognizable by a modern reader.

The working poor typically did not have the money nor the time for a leisurely luncheon of crumpets and wine. Many of them were left to go hungry until later in the day, if they could afford a second meal at all. In Mayhew's series, he notes the daily meals of his interviewees, and most did not eat lunch. If they did, it was something cheap and portable, like a boiled egg or a piece of bread.

Luncheon was often taken by the working professionals. Like today, they relied on fast serve establishments and food stalls for a quick bite to eat before heading back to the office grind. There were oyster bars, shellfish shops, and sandwich stores that catered more to their male clientele. Some sandwich places charged a set price and men could eat ham, beef, and tongue sandwiches from a tray and drink stout, Pale ale, wine, or sherry with it[3].

At home, the wives and children of the middle-class professionals often had a small meal made up of cold leftovers from the day before. There might be one or two additional new dishes that were easy for the maid or cook to prepare.

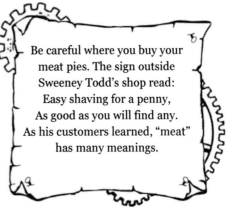

Be careful where you buy your meat pies. The sign outside Sweeney Todd's shop read: Easy shaving for a penny, As good as you will find any. As his customers learned, "meat" has many meanings.

Leftover meats from the previous day's supper would be consumed, such as game, poultry, ham, and hashed meats.

## At the End of the Day

Dinner was typically eaten any time between two and five o'clock, depending upon the number of daylight hours for the cooks to work with. Working middle-class families generally could take an hour's break for dinner, and could not linger over their plates like the rich did.

Some chophouses had sides available for purchase, such as cooked potatoes, ale, cheese, and pickles. Others might offer a slightly wider array of options for the middle-class palette, with a set number of courses or options. They might offer roasts, chops, pies, puddings, cheeses, and a variety of alcohols.

One famous period chophouse was called the Cheshire Cheese. For most of the day, men paid 2s.11d for an all-you-can-eat buffet of rump steak, pudding, and stewed cheese, and vegetables, and beer. The men who went weren't the very poor; someone like Mark's alter ego could afford to go[4].

Working poor families relied on cheap, but nutritious food during the work week. Foods that we'd consider old-fashion, stick-to-your-ribs food were the menu of choice. Split peas, corn, and grain all provided hot, hearty, and filling meals for pennies.

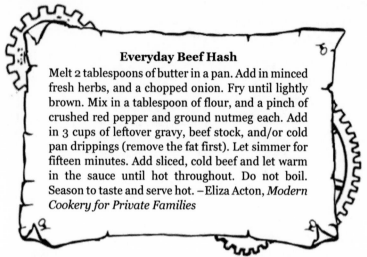

**Everyday Beef Hash**

Melt 2 tablespoons of butter in a pan. Add in minced fresh herbs, and a chopped onion. Fry until lightly brown. Mix in a tablespoon of flour, and a pinch of crushed red pepper and ground nutmeg each. Add in 3 cups of leftover gravy, beef stock, and/or cold pan drippings (remove the fat first). Let simmer for fifteen minutes. Add sliced, cold beef and let warm in the sauce until hot throughout. Do not boil. Season to taste and serve hot. –Eliza Acton, *Modern Cookery for Private Families*

Nearly everyone ate meat at least once a week, typically on Sunday if they couldn't afford it any other day. It might be a cheap roast, but it was just as likely to be a sheep's head or beef's liver. Families without cooking facilities could still have a hearty meat-based meal on Sunday by purchasing ready-made meat pies, puddings, and potatoes from the market. The local bakeries charged a small fee for baking these meals.

Since everyone needs vegetables and protein in their diets throughout the week and not just on Sundays, there are sneaky ways to get some into one's diet for cheap. You can arrange for shopping expeditions down to the market areas, either for your own heroine or her servant who has an eye for a bargain. Stale greens and small, dried pieces of cheese could be picked up at corner shops and costermongers at the end of the day for a discount. Tripe (stomach) shops sometimes sold their wares boiled so that it could be wrapped in paper and brought home, ready to eat. Cheap fish could be picked up down at Billingsgate after 6pm when the fish started to spoil[5].

Henry Mayhew noted bread and an onion was a popular dinner for labouring men. Can you imagine how bad some of those rooms much have stank, with the onion and beer farts every night? Eww. Mayhew also recommended that a family drink two pints of milk daily, though that was beyond the means of many.

A family like Martha's would have had enough to have a basic, but filling meal. On the weekend, they'd probably have a mutton roast, or a cheap cut of meat, like a calf's head or the organs. Liver was very nutritious, and a head had a lot of meat on it, once it was all picked off the bone. Potatoes increasingly became more and more important, but cabbage, turnips, and carrots were often very accessible and inexpensive. Dried green peas stored well, were very nutritious, and inexpensive. Just about anything boiled could have dried peas added and peas could replace meat when economy was necessary.

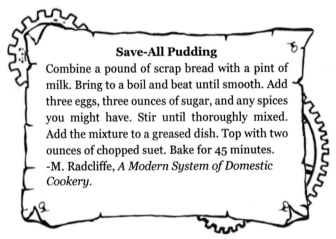

**Save-All Pudding**

Combine a pound of scrap bread with a pint of milk. Bring to a boil and beat until smooth. Add three eggs, three ounces of sugar, and any spices you might have. Stir until thoroughly mixed. Add the mixture to a greased dish. Top with two ounces of chopped suet. Bake for 45 minutes.
-M. Radcliffe, *A Modern System of Domestic Cookery*.

At the very end of the day was supper, which was another insubstantial snack. For the working class, that might have been nothing more than a slice of bread. For the gentry, it might have been cakes, breads, cold meats, and an array of leftovers similar to luncheon.

Men had more options for supper. Single heroes like Mark might rely on chophouses to cook their dinners and suppers, depending upon how busy they were that day. A bachelor with a little ready money could purchase a cut of cheap meat from a butcher. He'd then take that meat to the chophouse where they'd cook it for him. He'd be able to eat the meal there, kept company by other single gents, or men who'd been kicked out of their homes for bad behavior.

## Hunger, Famines, and the Potato

Bread and beer made up the bulk of the poor's diet. It was the main source of their fibre and carbohydrates, along with a bit of protein. As the 19th century chugged on, potatoes replaced bread as the mainstay in the poor's diet. It wasn't an overnight decision, but the result of a series of laws and changes in agriculture over a span of time.

There were already problems with food supply across Europe by the time Victoria took the throne. This was made even worse by a succession of potato blights. The potato was high in vitamin C and provided more calories per acre than any other food crop. It was perfect for feeding the poor. However, the total focus on it meant that places like Ireland were trapped by growing only one crop.

Before the blight, it was estimated that a whole third of Ireland's population depended on potatoes for 80% of their total diet[6].

By 1846, nearly 75% of the potato crop was lost. Losing the crop didn't just affect that year, but the successive ones, since there was no seed crop to set aside. Consequently, one million Irish died. And the British sat by for a goodly portion of that time and didn't do anything.

How will your heroine with poor Irish relations react when a wealthy suitor rambles off racist comments about the Irish? How angry will your upstart politician be, after labouring all day in the Commons for relief to be sent to Ireland, when his betrothed says the Irish deserved to die; they were just poor people anyway.

## Food in the Workhouse

If your heroine and her family are unfortunate enough to end up in a workhouse, the food they would eat would vary greatly. There was a lot of variation between the workhouses of the mid-1700s and the mid-1800s.

Most of us know about Oliver Twist asking for more, please, sir. In the 1750s, one parish workhouse fed the following to their inmates[7]:

- 7 oz. meat without bones
- 2 ounces butter
- 4 oz. cheese
- 1lb bread
- 3 pints beer

I ran this through a calorie tracker and came out to about 2600 calories a day. This is a decent amount of calories for someone who is busy. However, someone doing heavy labour would need closer to 3500-4000 calories per day. This menu is also low in some key nutrients, including calcium and Vitamin C, and could lead to a variety of health problems that would impact one's ability to work as they aged.

Eighty years later, we see less food in many workhouses. Meat and bacon once a week each. Three-quarters of a pound of potatoes two days a week. A couple of cups of running, thin gruel every day. A couple cups of soup once a week. Lots of bread. A bit of cheese every day.

But, really, 2 ounces of cheese and 7 ounces of bread really isn't a lot to eat for supper after outside working all day crushing rocks[8].

While one could not die of starvation on this diet, there is no doubt that plenty of people went to bed hungry at night.

## Food in Prison

Well, this is awkward. Mark nearly caught the traitor, but

unfortunately got accused of theft in the process. He'll get out in a few days, once someone informs the local magistrate of his unique and delicate situation. But, in the meantime, he'll get to suffer through the food at Newgate Prison.

Newgate wasn't a hotel, that's for sure, and the prison system of the Victorian Age was not kind. He's not a gentleman, so he can't even get a nice, private room. Instead, he's in a cell with the other common trash. Thankfully, though, our hero would not starve to death, though he might consider it an option.

For breakfast, Mark would be served eight ounces of bread (the ladies received six ounces) and a pint of oatmeal gruel that might be well watered down. He'll want to avoid any floating black spots; that's the rat droppings.

Oh, and in case you didn't know this: mouse droppings look like black sesame seeds. After a mice outbreak in my agency's kitchen, I've never been able to eat a black sesame seed again. And I'm happy to share that trauma with you.

Dinner was more varied, with half the week seeing three ounces of cooked meat (without the bone), more bread, and a half pound of potatoes. The other half would have Mark eating a pint of soup (mind the floaters!) and more bread. In theory, the soup should contain three ounces of meat with some vegetables. But these were prisoners and no one wanted to serve them good food. Otherwise, more would commit crimes just for the meals.

Supper that night would be the same as breakfast. Yum.

## Pulling it All Together

Do you need to stop and have a snack? I sure do after writing all that. Though, perhaps not the rat droppings. Still gagging a bit over that tidbit.

Most writers don't spend pages waxing on about the glories and horrors of dinner, and many readers are grateful for it. A light touch is often the best approach, but that doesn't mean food should be reduced to a monotonous line about eating and nothing else.

In a time where eating was still very much tied to the seasons and a succession of bad harvests could cause a nation-wide famine, a lot can be said with only a few comments about eating thin gruel, out-of-season cucumbers, and picking up a meat pie from a street vendor.

A lot can be said through someone's eating habits, without ever saying a word. Use mealtimes and food as a way to add an additional layer of texture, and leave the recipes to the cookbooks. Ask your characters some polite questions or interrogate them until they confess their secrets; examine who they are. Will Martha push her food around her plate, because

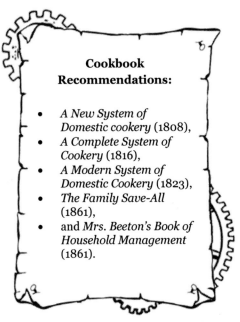

**Cookbook Recommendations:**

- *A New System of Domestic cookery* (1808),
- *A Complete System of Cookery* (1816),
- *A Modern System of Domestic Cookery* (1823),
- *The Family Save-All* (1861),
- and *Mrs. Beeton's Book of Household Management* (1861).

she'd rather go hungry than eat the ham that she knew had been covered in flies for days? Will Mark try to impose himself on any married coworkers and acquaintances for a dinner invitation, so that he can eat anywhere but at a chophouse by himself?

Do your servants steal from their lady whenever she sends them to the market, or does she pay them enough that they don't need to? Is your housekeeper constantly worried about the housemaids breaking into the larder and stuffing their faces with pastries, cheese, and cream?

What about onboard your steamship? Will the captain set out fair rations for everyone, or will rations be determined by rank? Will the captain only eat fresh food, while his or her shipmates eat rotting cabbage? That sounds like a mutiny waiting to happen.

Beyond shamelessly plugging my own food history book here, there are plenty of other resources available. There are a number of popular period cookbooks available online for free, so take advantage of their advice when deciding on what your own heroine serves her family for Sunday dinner. You might even find a few additional humorous calamities to enrich your heroine's world.

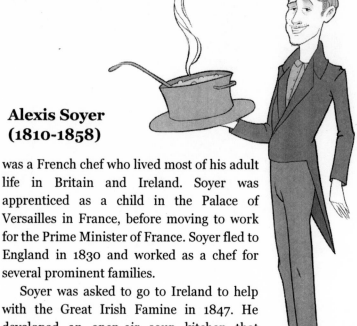

## Alexis Soyer (1810-1858)

was a French chef who lived most of his adult life in Britain and Ireland. Soyer was apprenticed as a child in the Palace of Versailles in France, before moving to work for the Prime Minister of France. Soyer fled to England in 1830 and worked as a chef for several prominent families.

Soyer was asked to go to Ireland to help with the Great Irish Famine in 1847. He developed an open-air soup kitchen that served thousands free of charge. At the height of the famine, it was said Soyer's kitchens served soup and a piece of bread to *twenty-six thousand people* every day. It was during this time that he penned *Soyer's Charitable Cookery* and donated the proceeds of his book to charity.

Soyer went on to write several other books, each focusing on a different social class and the challenges that each faced. He also travelled to the front during the Crimean War to advise the army on cooking and nutrition. He was also considered a cooking revolutionary, creating a small, portable stove (for those without cooking facilities), cooked with gas, had his own product line, and was basically a Victorian celebrity chef.

# Chapter 4: Charity Begins Anywhere but Here

*"I am in earnest. Go and buy (a turkey), and tell 'em to bring it here, that I may give them the direction where to take it. Come back with the man, and I'll give you a shilling. Come back with him in less than five minutes and I'll give you half-a-crown!"*

*The boy was off like a shot. He must have had a steady hand at a trigger who could have got a shot off half so fast.*

*"I'll send it to Bob Cratchit's!" whispered Scrooge, rubbing his hands, and splitting with a laugh.*

*-Ebenezer Scrooge (Charles Dickens, A Christmas Carol)*

I am under strict orders from my step-kids to not prattle on about my time working at a homeless agency during this chapter. My youngest has informed me that I am allowed to mention it during the section on soup kitchens, but nowhere else. Tall order, but I'm going to try!

Charity and poverty is rather complicated. On the one hand, there is the notion of good Christian charity throughout Georgian and Victorian times. A good Christian helps others in need. On the other hand, these same good Christians were still people. Many were convinced helping the poor meant that they'd give up working all together and rely on handouts. Thank goodness that thinking died out with Queen Victoria, right?

There was no old age security, employment insurance,

worker's compensation, and disability insurance. People were left to their own devices. Some people were born into poverty and that's just where they will end up.

However, too many impoverished people starving to death was a revolution waiting to happen. Plus, again, Christian charity. So there were various forms of assistance during this period, even if the projects were degrading, cruel, and violent.

## State-Run Charity & Poor Law

To understand the charity and social safety net that existed in Georgian and Victorian times, you'll need a quick course in the Poor Laws. There were a lot of them, so I'm going to summarize them down to just a few bullet points.

I use the term "state" in this section, even though the bulk of the charity I'm about to describe is parish-based. Parishes were territorial divisions within the country looked after by the Church of England. Parishes were responsible for the poor in their area and Parish law was designed to ensure some security existed for the very poor and destitute. Like today, wealthy parishes are situated in wealthy areas, whereas the poor ones exist in the places where the wealth is needed the most.

What people considered "poor" and "destitute" varied and plenty of underfunded, overwhelmed parishes rejected help for blind women in their eighties and physically deformed young men.

By 1722, the parishes were allowed to build workhouses; they weren't required for another century. The parish system was well known to be corrupt and notoriously stingy. They spent their efforts tracking down anyone who could pay for the people under their charge. To claim the help of the parish, a person had to prove they lived there, and they tried any trick to "prove" an individual in need didn't belong to the parish.

Poor parishes were known to pay impoverished bachelors in other parishes a fee (40s, or £3.3s, mid-18th century) to marry some of their poor women. This might seem counterproductive as a cost-savings method, but the marriage forced the woman to move to her new husband's parish. Which meant, they were someone else's problem.

Can you imagine being a nineteen-year-old orphan, unable to work due to a lingering illness, and then married off to some strange man and forced to move to live with him? And, if she didn't move, well, she wouldn't get any more money because they tried to provide for her and she refused the help.

I was shocked to discover that a law had to be passed in 1772 that prevented moving a woman in labour. It seems like a weird law to pass; why would anyone move a woman with contractions? Because, some parishes were known to push a woman in labour across the parish boundary so that her child was someone else's problem.

Literally pushed her.

Children born into the tender care of a parish didn't have good prospects. For example, St. Luke's parish poorhouse received 53 children between 1750 and 1755. By 1755, all of children had died. In another thirteen parishes during the same time period, 2239 children were born or admitted into parish care. 1074 were eventually discharged for various reasons. Of the remaining 1165, only 168 were alive in 1755.

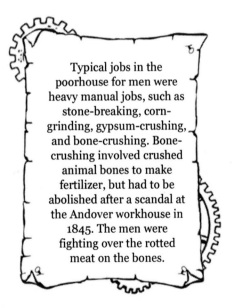

Typical jobs in the poorhouse for men were heavy manual jobs, such as stone-breaking, corn-grinding, gypsum-crushing, and bone-crushing. Bone-crushing involved crushed animal bones to make fertilizer, but had to be abolished after a scandal at the Andover workhouse in 1845. The men were fighting over the rotted meat on the bones.

It had been thought that the number of deaths was an exaggeration, but it was soon clear they were not. These bastard and orphan children were not being looked after properly and Parliament was forced to act. A series of laws were passed starting in 1762 that required parishes to provide proper care for infants and small children. From that point on, parish children under the age of six were sent to the country to live with paid nurses, who made a bonus of 10s for every baby who survived their care.

These were acts passed to keep babies alive[1].

A big change happened in 1834. That was when the new Poor Law came into effect. It was designed to, as the National Archives puts it, "reduce the cost of looking after the poor, prevent scroungers, and impose a system which would be the same all over the country[2]."

This law is where we start to see the horrible workhouses cropping up. Poor people could now only get help if they went into the workhouse. So the workhouse conditions were horrible on purpose to discourage people from asking for help.

It took several scandals to have the laws reformed again before the poor and desperate were not treated like criminals.

## Individual Charity

People were treated appallingly in this period. Children were left to die in the streets and up chimneys, teenage girls were left to die of mercury poisoning and syphilis, and disabled men to drag themselves along by their knees and elbows begging for their suppers. Yet, everyone claimed Christian virtue. It was preached from the pulpit and written about in cookbooks and domestic guides. That is where the contradiction lies and can be difficult for a modern reader to grasp.

In Jane Austen's *Emma*, Miss Bates and her mother, Mrs. Bates, are poor. Once respectable members of the population, the death of Mr. Bates left the women barely able to afford the apothecary to care for their ailments. Emma Woodhouse, the rich heroine of the book, gives them a hind quarter of pork, which was a significant amount of meat, for them to have salted and cured. Mr. Knightley, likewise the rich hero, gives them a bushel of fresh apples from his storeroom.

All of this kindness is lovely, but why didn't they ever offer to pay Mrs. Bates's medical bills or provide the ladies with a cottage to live in rent-free? Perhaps the Bateses wouldn't have accepted it, so gifts of food was all the rich members of the village could provide, but I've always been left with the nagging feeling of the contradictory.

Helping one's neighbours in need was an expectation of upper-class households, for sure, but also for the wealthier members of the middle-class. This was always true, but it became more noticeable and public as the evangelical movement grew in the 19th century. Converts wanted to express their faith and saw charity as a call to arms.

Mrs. Rundell, one of our period experts for this book, said that "some part of every person's fortune should be devoted to charity." I can get behind that.

And maybe I'm judging Emma and Mr. Knightley too severely.

Rundell's suggestions for the poor generally deal with giving them food, which makes sense. As we've seen, food is a major expense in terms of time, fuel, and money. Giving a present of a home prepared and cooked meal would be a welcome treat for anyone, but especially a woman lying-in with her eighth baby and her eldest daughter sick with pneumonia.

I've cooked many of Rundell's suggestions and have found them to be surprisingly filling. She recommends cooking a rice pudding in a cooling oven. I successfully did that with a modern oven, though I did have to soak my rice first, since my oven doesn't retain its heat nearly as well as an old cast iron stove would.

She also suggests a jug of skimmed milk. She notes that this is a very common present for the poor in the country, which would make sense. Ready access to milk would be easy enough for any well-to-do land owner, who could arrange for the dairy to distribute the milk once the cream had been skimmed off.

The old standbys are in her book, including soup. She recommends adding vegetables which "will afford better nourishment than the laborious poor can obtain; especially as they are rarely tolerable cooks, and have not the fuel to do justice to what they buy." Ignoring that little dig about their cooking skills, she does recognize that fuel was an important hindrance to proper nutrition.

Mrs. Radcliffe and Mrs. Rundell both recommend making a large pot of soup while cooking other things, such as baking bread and cooking the soup alongside in the oven. It economized on fuel, which was a big expense, and the meals were acceptable to give to the poor. They both felt it was a good use of bones, and added little expense. Rundell said:

> If in the villages about London, abounding with opulent families, the quantity of ten gallons were made in ten gentlemen's houses, there would be a hundred gallons of wholesome agreeable food given weekly for the supply of forty poor families, at the rate of two gallons and a half each. What a relief to the laboring husband, instead of bread and cheese, to have a warm comfortable meal!

I think proper Mrs. Rundell was a subversive at heart!

Mrs. Radcliffe likewise agreed in her cookbook (about the soup, not the subversion), saying that:

> this will open a new source to those benevolent housekeepers, who are disposed to relieve the poor, and will show the industrious classes how much they have it in their power to assist themselves, and rescue them from being objects of charity dependent on the precarious bounty of others, by teaching them how they may obtain a cheap, abundant, salubrious, and agreeable aliment for themselves and families.

I can see Martha picking up a book similar to Mrs. Rundell's from her mistress's personal library. She takes the charity sections to heart and asks her mistress if they should be doing more to help the poor in their neighbourhood. Said in the right way, only the most cold-hearted of mistresses would refuse to arrange with her cook for an additional soup to be made weekly for the old, sickly widow down the road.

One of the easiest ways to show someone's character is to show their attitudes on charity. The loud and boisterous who announce each good will they do often don't do a lot that helps others. Some people are very quiet or even donate anonymously, not wanting anything traced back to them. Others think people should pull themselves up by their bootstraps or some such.

## Soup Kitchens

As the Industrial Revolution progressed and the population of Britain grew by leaps and bounds, London was under great pressure. The evangelical movement was chugging along full-speed and many of those took up the cause of helping the less fortunate as a means of dedication to their faith. Also, many middle-class and wealthier individuals wanted to do more, to help those in need. With rampant hunger throughout London, soup kitchens began popping up.

The poor and working class often had no way to cook, so they spent a good portion of their wages on street food or retailers who sold leftover food from inns and hotels for 4d to 8d. For the very poor and destitute, that was often too much on some days. Soup kitchens, which served bread and soup, became increasingly necessary. Leicester Square fed 200-300 people daily at theirs, while Farrington Street fed 8000-10,000 people daily in the mid-century[3].

Alexis Soyer (1810-1858) was a popular French chef in Britain. He is credited with inventing the soup kitchens used in Ireland and Britain. I was struck by Soyer's proud description of how to run a soup kitchen and I had a number of flashbacks to when I was in charge of an inner city agency's meal program. Six nights a week, we served a hot meal to 200-400 people. The quality and quantity varied, though I worked very hard to educate the volunteer meal groups on healthy, nutritional options. It was a struggle and, it seemed in Soyer's time, it was for him, too.

It's interesting that Soyer and I had the same complaints: healthy food was necessary. Malnutrition was dangerous and debilitating. Warm, nutritious, and hearty food is a necessity of life.

Many Victorian soup kitchens were outside, for the best air circulation and to avoid the spread of disease. Imagine the humiliation of a former middle class woman having been reduced to standing in line for her food . . . only to see an old school pal at the front organizing the charity. That's the making of an awkward scene.

Soyer recommended giving people ten minutes to eat before they were asked to move along to allow others in to be served. I have personal experience at asking people to move along and, let me tell you, it isn't nearly as easy as Soyer makes it sound. Consider for a moment that you've stood in line, in the snow, for over an hour to be near the front of the line. You aren't dressed properly for the weather. You finally get to sit down to your litre of soup and a hunk of bread, which might be too hot for you to eat without burning your tongue. Your hands are shaking, so you're spilling the soup on the table and on yourself.

And then some redhead in a bad mood wearing a staff shirt stands up on a chair and shouts that the line outside is around the corner and everyone has to hurry up their meal and get out.

I may or may not be that redhead in question.

*Cough.*

That's enough to cause a fight right there. Add in varying degrees of sobriety and a potentially unsafe situation can break out in a matter of moments. How will your upper-class social justice warrior cope with men swearing and pushing each other? Will she faint at the first sight of blood from a split lip? Or will she hike up her skirts, grab a hot soup spoon, and brain the first aggressor she can find?

What about someone like Mark? Will he jump in there, pulling people apart and shouting at them? Or has he seen enough fights at 2am in Covent Garden to know to stay out of it until someone's unconscious?

Soyer and various magazines, including *The Gentlemen's Magazine* (a century before), distributed recipes for families in need. They weren't meant or designed for the poor to cook themselves. Rather, they were designed for the wealthy to cook and to bring to those in need, either as a gift to an individual family or as an organized event[4].

I decided to cook two of Soyer's recipes to feed to my family. I picked his "Receipt No. 1 – For Two Gallons." He put the price at 6d, which would have been very inexpensive for a solidly middle-class family to make up once a week. In fact, the ingredients today only cost me in the $7 range—and it was a lot of soup!

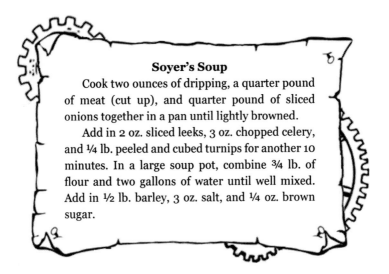

**Soyer's Soup**
Cook two ounces of dripping, a quarter pound of meat (cut up), and quarter pound of sliced onions together in a pan until lightly browned.
Add in 2 oz. sliced leeks, 3 oz. chopped celery, and ¼ lb. peeled and cubed turnips for another 10 minutes. In a large soup pot, combine ¾ lb. of flour and two gallons of water until well mixed. Add in ½ lb. barley, 3 oz. salt, and ¼ oz. brown sugar.

I picked this specific recipe because Soyer bragged that, "The above soup has been tasted by numerous noblemen, members of parliament, and several ladies who have lately visited my kitchen department, and who have considered it very good and nourishing." You know what? It was a bit lumpier than I prefer my soup (the flour makes it closer to a thin gravy), and a bit saltier than I'm used to. But it was surprisingly good and quite filling.

Then I tried his Meager Peas Soup for when the kitchens couldn't afford to purchase meat. Soyer felt the combination of ingredients would "act generously on the digestive organs, particularly to a stomach which has suffered from want of food."

I'm not sure about the generosity of the soup on my organs, but it was surprisingly delicious. My kids were mopping up every drop in their bowls with the buns I made. It didn't leftover well. The flour made the soup rather gloppy, but some extra broth stirred in during the re-heating stage fixed it all up!

Always trust a French chef.

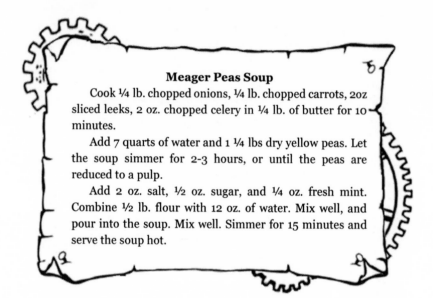

### Meager Peas Soup

Cook ¼ lb. chopped onions, ¼ lb. chopped carrots, 2oz sliced leeks, 2 oz. chopped celery in ¼ lb. of butter for 10 minutes.

Add 7 quarts of water and 1 ¼ lbs dry yellow peas. Let the soup simmer for 2-3 hours, or until the peas are reduced to a pulp.

Add 2 oz. salt, ½ oz. sugar, and ¼ oz. fresh mint. Combine ½ lb. flour with 12 oz. of water. Mix well, and pour into the soup. Mix well. Simmer for 15 minutes and serve the soup hot.

## Hannah Snell
## (1723-1792)

Hannah Snell was a female soldier who enlisted into the army under the name of James Grey. Hannah had survived with her identity intact during a flogging by, in her words, taking off her shirt and pressing against a gate.

She eventually joined the Marines and was nicknamed Molly. That nickname says a lot, since Molly was the name for effeminate boys or homosexual men. Chances are, at least some of them knew she was a woman. Ever a troublemaker, she was sentenced to another flogging while onboard. That time, she was permitted to wear a large scarf around her neck during the flogging, which covered her chest.

Eventually, her soldiering days were done. The Royal Hospital admitted her to the pension list with the standard 5d per day pension, due to being injured in action.

Unfortunately, she ended up suffering from an unknown affliction and died in Bedlam Hospital in 1792.

# Chapter 5: Respectable Professionals

*"There are a set of religious, or rather moral writers, who teach that virtue is the certain road to happiness, and vice to misery, in this world. A very wholesome and comfortable doctrine, and to which we have but one objection, namely, that it is not true."*
-Henry Fielding, *The History of Tom Jones, a Foundling*

The next few chapters are dedicated to the career paths available to Londoners. This is by no means an exhaustive list; it took Henry Mayhew four volumes just to write about the outdoor jobs people had in the Victorian Age!

Social rank was everything until the Industrial Revolution, and it still meant a lot after the Revolution. Land meant wealth and consequence. A good landowner treated his tenants and servants like part of the business family. Bad land owners treated their employees like every horrible boss you've ever had.

Only a few ever inherited the giant estates and thousands of acres of land. Many more inherited a small cottage and a few dozen acres of land. Still others got an annuity (an annual allowance paid from the interest on a principle sum). Everyone else got a slap in the face and told to make their own way.

Not everyone was scrubbing the floors to pay the rent. There were a number of opportunities for even the high and mighty second (third, fourth . . .) sons of aristocrats to earn a living.

# The Paper Pushers

Not every Londoner was poor and struggling. There were plenty of professional jobs that we'd recognize today. One of the most important professional jobs was the clerk. There were tens of thousands of them throughout England and their numbers grew annually as business flourished. The clerk job was a skilled position; it required a solid grasp of writing and reading, plus arithmetic skills. There were opportunities in the government sector, as well as the private sector.

Mark would think himself way too good for a clerk's office; that involved work. Covert missions while posing as a clerk were his style. However, the clerk's office would be a good place for a younger, less snotty version of Mark. We'll pretend that is Mark's brother, John.

With an education, John could get a job at the Post Office. They employed a few dozen clerks and they needed more as their service grew with the railways. The Bank of England employed hundreds of clerks. Once the railway companies began laying track, they needed clerks to contain the massive paper trail of work, and employed about a thousand people just for paperwork.

I was surprised to discover that the huge breweries all needed a couple dozen clerks each for all of their accounting and filing needs.

The job descriptions varied a little, depending upon the job requirements. There were some common tasks. Clerks wrote and copied letters, filed the copies, and posted the originals. Ledgers had to be kept up to date with the dates of letters being mailed out.

They were basically a combination of email, spreadsheets, and calendars, only breathing.

Clerks also worked what we'd today call banker's hours; one little girl wrote that her father worked from 10am to 4pm. She noted in her diary that her father was required to look nice for his job, complete with a good quality hat, so he spent more money on clothes than a labourer or a more typical worker in his salary class. However, his reduced hours meant he had time to work odd jobs around the neighbourhood to bring in extra funds.

The income of clerks did range widely. At the top, an assistant secretary in the Post Office made £700-£800 (1839). The lower clerks, "junior clerk 2nd class," were making in the range of £90-£100. While not major money, it was enough to afford a decent set of rooms and put food on the table, especially if one's children and wife were working. That income would push someone into the lower ranks of the middle-class, offering some marrying social mobility for one's daughters.

The Bank of England was comparable to the Post Office. The Governor only made £400 a year, which surprised me; I was expecting it to be at least double or triple that, considering what his job entailed.

Until 1844, the bank clerks under the age of 21 were paid on a sliding scale. If they started at seventeen, they began with an income of £10. But, each year it was increased until it was £50 at age twenty-one. That wasn't a lot for a young man, and he'd most likely still live at home with those wages. After 1844, the wage was updated to £100 for those at twenty-one, at least. A bank clerk also had the opportunity to rise to £250 later in life, which was a comfortable, middle-class wage.

The clerk position wasn't something that an upper-class family would tolerate for their own children. It would plunge them down too far. Instead, it was an excellent job for a son trying to rise beyond his working class roots, provided they were able to afford his education. For a grateful son (basically someone not Mark), a clerk position would be a major coup. He could earn the same money as his father, but only work six to eight hours a day. He could be available to help his parents, and later his wife, with chores, and might even pick up the occasional odd job on the side.

## The Legal Eagles

The law was always a popular choice with many of the educated regardless of rank. There were two types of lawyers, attracting men from different social classes. At the top were the barristers. They were very respectable, and often quite well off. They argued cases in court, using their wit and education to defend or prosecute.

It's why Edward Ferrars in *Sense and Sensibility* said:

> The law was allowed to be genteel enough; many
> young men, who had chambers in the Temple, made
> a very good appearance in the first circles, and drove
> about town in very knowing gigs.

He was from an upper class, wealthy family, but he was a younger son with no occupation. His family were fine with him entering the law; it was genteel enough for them.

Barristers weren't the only aspect of law. Below them were a host of others types of lawyers: solicitors, attorneys, and proctors. They were hired by clients, and they did the grunt work, but anything that required going to court was hired out to the barrister. Solicitor, attorneys, and proctors were the lower class of lawyer, and consequently the lower class of person.

This seems like a fine point to a modern reader, but it was quite important in Georgian times. Barristers didn't take money directly from clients, so they were not in trade. They were solely dependent upon attorneys and solicitors for cases, and not the common rabble.

This very fine point meant that the barrister was a respectable job and something that the younger son of a gentleman would be likely to do. A family desperate to move up in ranks might put their cleverest son through school and university just so that he could get a barrister position, thereby climbing the ranks. It's also why Caroline Bingley mocked Jane Bennet who had an attorney uncle; the attorney was middle-class and well beneath Caroline.

All of this got tossed out the window by the 1870s, when the legal system got a massive reorganization. Attorneys were done away with, as were many other roles, and all that were left were barristers and solicitors.

## Take This & Call Me in the Morning

I'm Canadian. I've lived my entire life with universal health care. I get sick? I go to the doctor. I get really sick? I go to the hospital. The internet tells me I'm spoiled rotten. I tend to agree.

Medicine cost money in Georgian and Victorian times. Most people couldn't afford treatment, and were nursed at home by women. Many of the cookbooks and domestic guides written during the 18th and 19th centuries have sections about homemade cures for various ailments.

Some ailments couldn't be cured at home with rosemary and sage oils. Either you suffered in silence (as many did), suffered loudly (as I'm sure many more did), or hoped you were wealthy enough to afford the medical care.

The medical profession varied, with wildly different incomes and status. At the very bottom were the apothecaries. They were druggists, and allowed to prescribe, prepare, and sell medications. Many areas did not have a physician, so the apothecary took over the role. He was allowed, provided he did not charge for his medical advice; just his drugs.

The drugs themselves were expensive, and might contain rather dangerous or addictive substances. Since the apothecary sold medicines, he was considered in trade, so could never break the upper-class ceiling.

Surgeons were the people who did work. They operated on people, dealt with skin diseases, STIs, and anything that couldn't be cured with a drug or tonic. Until 1745, surgeons were linked with barbers, and surgeons used corpses from graveyards to practice on. They were seen as similar to labourers.

Surgeons were decently educated, and had been apprenticed since their early teens for three to seven years. They could either then be freelancers, or go on to write the exams to become members of the Company of Surgeons (after 1745). Some surgeons had medical degrees, as Edinburgh and Paris were centres of surgical learning at the time. The Royal Navy and the army hired surgeons, as they needed people with experience and who weren't afraid to hack off a festering limb.

The surgeon's social standing didn't begin its elevation until the end of the Victorian age.

Physicians were at the top of respectability and fees. Physicians were the most expensive and considered the best of the best. They did not do anything that involved touching patients beyond taking a pulse. They did "physic;" that is, they gave people drugs. Lots and lots and lots of drugs.

A physician had to be licenced. To become a fellow of the Royal College of Physicians, a man had to belong to the Church of England, graduate Cambridge or Oxford where they received no practical training. For that, they went to Edinburgh and could charge even more with that practice on their resume.

Physicians weren't a huge portion of the medical professionals and most of them hung out in the London area, where there were more rich people to afford outrageous prices for medicine often more damaging than the illness.

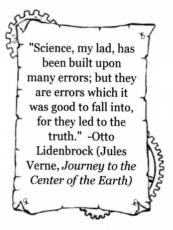

"Science, my lad, has been built upon many errors; but they are errors which it was good to fall into, for they led to the truth." -Otto Lidenbrock (Jules Verne, *Journey to the Center of the Earth*)

# Mad Scientists and Madder Professors

The Victorian era was an incredible time for scientists, tinkerers, inventors, and dreamers. Assuming they had financial backing, of course. But that's what parents and gambling are for.

After centuries of small, slow-progressing technologies, they reached a watershed moment in the Victorian age. Soon, new inventions seemed to be developed weekly.

Before people become lawyers and doctors, inventors and

tinkerers, they often went to university. Oxford and Cambridge were the choices, where you could rub shoulders with future prime ministers, judges, and country squires who all had sisters to marry off.

University learning wasn't the same as the education today. Tutors looked after the education. These tutors were called fellows: undergraduates who were elected to the permanent membership because they'd scored well on their undergrad exams. (I'm simplifying here). Becoming a fellow had benefits, including an annual stipend.

Ladies were barred from the higher halls of learning for most of the Victorian era. Academic halls for women were eventually established in Cambridge (1869) and Oxford (1878), but it wouldn't be until the 20th century that the segregation of the sexes ended.

But not all of the great Victorian inventors had formal education. Books and the lecture circuit provided the curious with exposure to new ideas. This is where you can get around pesky issues like women not allowed into universities or men being too poor to attend university.

Michael Faraday is a great example of this. He is known as one of the most influential scientists in history. In fact, anyone who's read the *Dresden Files* will have learned about the Faraday Cage (though, granted, it was talking about magic as opposed to electricity, but look, I'm a slow learner). But despite all of Faraday's accomplishments (and many I don't even understand), he wasn't

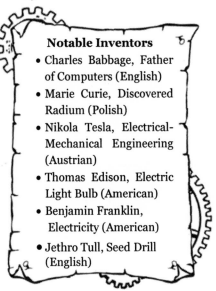

**Notable Inventors**
- Charles Babbage, Father of Computers (English)
- Marie Curie, Discovered Radium (Polish)
- Nikola Tesla, Electrical-Mechanical Engineering (Austrian)
- Thomas Edison, Electric Light Bulb (American)
- Benjamin Franklin, Electricity (American)
- Jethro Tull, Seed Drill (English)

well educated in a formal sense.

Michael Faraday's parents couldn't afford more than a basic education for him and he had to be apprenticed out by fourteen to a bookbinder and bookseller. Through his apprenticeship, he became self-taught in science. He attended lectures, got assistant positions, and surrounded himself with scientists.

"I often say that when you can measure what you are speaking about, and express it in numbers, you know something about it; but when you cannot express it in numbers, your knowledge is of a meagre and unsatisfactory kind." – William Thomson, First Lord Kelvin[2]

He was treated horribly, as he wasn't a gentleman, but he stuck it out and learned. He overcame his lack of formal education and social prejudice, and made some of the most important scientific discoveries of his era.

Likewise, your upper-middle class or even wealthy lady with an interest in science could still make her own path. Georgiana Cavendish was one of

A Faraday Cage

the richest women in England, assuming you didn't take her gambling debts into account. She developed a keen interest in mineralogy and chemistry in the 1790s, decades before a woman could study this at the university level. But she attended chemistry lectures at the Royal Academy, set up a small lab at Devonshire House to do chemical experiments, and studied minerals and fossils.

Her knowledge and interest in chemistry and mineralogy led her to become patron to several struggling scientists, including Dr. Thomas Beddoes, who went on to discover laughing gas[3].

So there's no excuse for your rich widow not to indulge in chemical experiments in her kitchen. She might discover a new chemical that changes everything.

# Holy Men

If nothing else, you can always become a preacher. Today, preachers are people who feel that is their calling. In Regency times, things were rather different. The Church of England was the established religion of the era. The Church held great power and influence, and therefore it was acceptable for the younger sons of gentlemen and solidly middle-class individuals to become vicars of local parishes.

The local parish was run by the parish priest; they were the vicar, rector, or curate. He preached on Sundays, visited the sick, and would officiate important events like funerals and weddings. The job position was known as "a living." He received all or at least a good part of the local tithes until 1840. After, the minister was given a payment equal to one-tenth of the farm produce in the area.

They also got farmland that came with the parsonage house itself. Jane Austen's father raised animals on his land to help support his large family. It's probably why Austen writes so much about vicars; she lived with one!

Some of the parish livings were passed into the hands of the local landowners, who gave the livings to people they deemed worthy, such as their closest relations. In 1830, over 7000 of the 11,000 or so livings in England and Wales were controlled by private parties, such as rich landowners.

The minister didn't need a religious calling to be a clergyman; it was a profession. Clergymen could make anywhere from £100 to £1000 a year in the Regency era, so getting a good living was obviously important. However, income could be raised by farming, or by taking on students to private tutor, as Austen's father did.

Mark's mother once suggested he become a clergyman, but even he felt a gambler shouldn't be a vicar. Martha's brothers would have had a harder time being even a lowly curate due to the colour of their skin.

## For King/Queen and Country

Britain was involved in numerous conflicts in the 18th and 19th centuries. There are the ones most people recognize, such as the Napoleonic Wars (various conflicts 1803-1815) and the American Revolutionary War (1775-1783). But Britain fought in many more, including the at-home conflicts of the Jacobite Rebellions (1715-16, 1745-46). There was a lot of fighting going on and people were needed to do it.

There was plenty of opportunity for work, provided you were okay with being shot or drowning. The army officer ranks were purchased, meaning those wanting those positions without working a couple of decades to earn them paid out a set amount of cash. This obviously attracted men of fortune, such as second sons who did not have a mansion and its inheritance to look forward to.

A family of servants making £30 a year could never pay the £1200 *and higher* fees for a commission in the Horse Guards. However, the 1s or so a day income of the regular rank and file was more than many of the young men were making back home. That doesn't even take into consideration whatever they could steal off corpses or plunder from conquered villages.

The food was awful, but no one joins the military for gourmet meals. Until 1847, enlistment was for life, so it wasn't for everyone. Because of that, the army had to use signing bonuses and trickery to get young men to sign up and follow the drum. In times of conflict, the old "sign up or go to prison" option for petty thieves was an inducement.

These are just some of the major conflicts that took place during the Georgian and Victorian ages:

- Seven Years' War (1756-1763)
- French Revolutionary Wars (1793-1802)
- Australian Frontier Wars (1788-1930)
- War of 1812 (1812-1815)
- Crimean War (1864-1856)
- Anglo-Zulu War (1879)
- Boer Wars (1880-1881, 1899-1902)
- Boxer Rebellion (1900)

Going to sea was also a difficult decision, but it could lead to money and social advancement, provided one came out of it with their body and mind intact. Samuel Johnson said men would rather go to prison than to sea, and "being in a ship is being in a jail with the chance of being drowned[4]."

It's little wonder that people needed to be . . . encouraged to join the navy. Press-gangs were legally permitted to force men and boys into the navy, literally seizing them from the streets. Impressment was said to be a legalized form of slavery, by the British against the British.

Impressment dates back to Elizabethan times and (later) the Vagrancy Act of 1597, where homeless people could be drafted into service. An act was passed in 1703 limiting impressment to adults only, exempting apprentices. In 1740, the minimum age was raised to fifty-five. But while technically a man of forty, let's say, couldn't be impressed after 1740, it didn't mean it still wasn't happening. One of the contributing causes to the War of 1812 was the impressment of Americans into the British Navy.

Pressed individuals had a great choice: they were allowed to sign up as a volunteer, thereby getting an advance and pay, or they were given nothing and still forced to go.

I'm not sure how this is a choice.

Impressment was last used during the Napoleonic Wars of 1803-1815, though it was never officially taken off the books until the 20th century, where it was replaced with conscription during World War I. So while Mark never had to worry about being pressed into the navy, Martha's mother might spend a lot of worry over one of her boys being forced into service[5].

Impressment crops up a lot in 18th century literature. Even the devilish rake Tom Jones (the good-looking bastard, not the good-looking singer) ran afoul of the press-gang in *Tom Jones*. His enemies bribed the local press-gang to target him, in hopes to drive him to sea and away from his heart's affection, Miss Sophia Weston. In *Fanny Hill*, Fanny's lover, Charles, goes missing. Years later she discovered that Charles's own father had him kidnapped and dragged away on a ship.

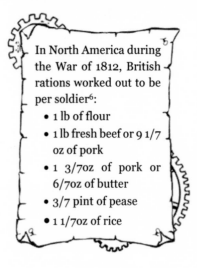

In North America during the War of 1812, British rations worked out to be per soldier[6]:

- 1 lb of flour
- 1 lb fresh beef or 9 1/7 oz of pork
- 1 3/7oz of pork or 6/7oz of butter
- 3/7 pint of pease
- 1 1/7oz of rice

These are great fictional points of drama, but it was a legitimate fear for any young man without friends and connections. Press-gangs caused obvious fear and anxiety in port towns, including London; it wasn't safe to go to any port town.

Many writers comment on the scurvy for the poor at sea, but the urban poor had no better access to Vitamin C than those onboard ship, until potatoes eventually substituted bread as the mainstay of the poor's diet. The low ranks of the army got rations, plus the occasional rabbit or any locally-purchased food (General Wellington frowned on stealing from allies when marching through their land). The navy had access to citrus fruits whenever they were in the warmer ports.

The navy also offered even greater opportunity for travel and bonuses. Capturing enemy ships or pirate vessels would trickle down the wealth to even the lowest crew member. They might not being home £30,000 like Captain Wentworth, but £50 or £100 would be a lot of money for someone who grew up making 5d a day running errands and chopping wood.

## Georgiana Cavendish, Duchess of Devonshire (1757 – 1808)

The lifestyle of a woman like Georgiana was as unattainable as touching the moon for nearly all of England's population. Her lifestyle would not have been possible without the endless and tireless work of her multitude of household staff, tradesmen and women, and professionals.

She was known in her own lifetime as the Empress of Fashion and the most respected woman of the Whig party. She married a man she barely knew at sixteen with no other goal in mind than to please him.

Though she could not run for office, she campaigned in the streets for others. She hosted lavish parties and events for the Whig party at home.

Georgiana's wealth couldn't buy her happiness. She had a gambling addiction and racked up such huge debts that bankrupting the estate wouldn't have paid them off. She turned to drugs and alcohol and suffered from bulimia.

While all of the people in this chapter would have done most anything to have Georgiana's money, her life showed that it could buy a full stomach, but not much else[1].

# Chapter 6: The View from Upstairs

*"The life of a gentleman's servant is something like that of a bird shut up in a cage. The bird is well housed and well fed, but deprived of liberty, and liberty is the dearest and sweetest object of all Englishmen."*
-William Tayler, footman (1837)

I have certain expectations from a Regency novel. First, I want parties. I don't care if they are grand balls or private dinners, I want the parties. Second, I want dresses. I'm generally a happy camper so long as I get a pretty dress dancing around a tight pair of wool trousers.

After all, the party is the quintessential image of the Regency era. Not to be outdone, the Victorians embraced the naughty waltz and turned dinner parties into an even snobbier art form than previous generations. Plus, the waist-shaping corsets and crinolines were back in style. It must have been an amazing sight: silks and taffetas all spinning and skipping around. A kaleidoscope of colours and textures. It must have been the peak of human culture and civilization.

Unless, of course, you were the poor sap scraping candle wax off the floor the morning after or in the kitchen scrubbing burnt pots. Life probably wasn't all that exciting for those folks. Because, the glamorous, beautiful, mystical world of the Regency and the Steampunk would not have existed without the unrelenting work of servants.

As the Regency elegance ended and the Victorian sensibility began, one in fifteen London dwellers were employed in some form of domestic service. As the 19th century progressed, the industrial revolution created wealth for many individuals who'd not had it before. By the 1850s, 750,000 women across Britain were domestic servants. By 1890, that number rose to 1.3 *million*[2]. There was a servant boom, employing all ages to do the endless list of menial tasks that still existed alongside the world of steam. This servant boom wouldn't fall below the million mark until the 1930s[3].

The most pressing question is why on earth so many servants were needed. The population was booming, sure, but it wasn't booming that much. There are a few reasons. The most obvious was that everyone needed help with daily chores. Even the poor needed help now and then to get their own work done. Servants were a means of showing off, a mark of one's social status. Finally, the Industrial Revolution provided a higher standard of living for many businessmen, who opted to hire someone to clean their boots instead of doing it themselves.

Isabella Beeton set out a recommendation chart for the middle class and upwardly mobile to help them judge how many servants they needed. Those making £150-£200 per annum should keep a maid-of-all-work and bring in a girl for occasional work. The £300 bracket could afford a maid-of-all-work and a nurserymaid. The £500 a year family could afford a cook, a housemaid, and a nursemaid. The £750 households could not get by without a cook, a housemaid, nursemaid, and a footboy. Finally, the £1000 year per annum households required a cook, upper and under housemaids, nursemaid, and a man servant.

When writing an upper class housewife, it's best to think of her as a businesswoman and treat her accordingly. Her duties are best comparable to running a modern-day small business, with anywhere from a couple to a couple dozen employees. It was a full-time job to run a household and it kept a woman very busy if she wanted to be the ideal mistress who ran an "orderly, vermin-free, sweet-smelling house.[4]" A successful household required a firm direction from which the servants received their orders.

Servants have long been cast as second-class citizens in books and costume dramas. When (some) modern commentaries discuss the history of the "career" women, the working women of the past are often forgotten. It's almost as though these women weren't real women.

One thing that bothers me about a lot of books based on these eras is the poor-but-not-poor heroines. The heroine has come on hard times, typically because of the actions of another, and is living in reduced circumstances. She's taken a couple of her old servants with her, and is left to support these elderly women who are beyond their working years.

This heroine seems to have enough time to dress up in fancy gowns and break into private parties to meet the man of her dreams, yet she never does a moment's housekeeping. She doesn't hire anyone, because she's broke, but somehow manages to have a spotless house when he comes to visit. Or the energy to spurn his advances. Or to say yes to his advances.

Whereas, by the time you're done reading this chapter, you'll wonder how anyone had time to eat or drink, let alone flirt at a ball!

It's impossible to make statements about the number of servants a household had, since it varied so much from house to house, and their own unique particular needs. Very poor households might hire day help or even a once-a-week helper, and send out some of the chores such as laundry. A small household with limited funds might only have a maid-of-all-work living with them. A middle-class home of a professional might have a cook, a housemaid, a nurse for the children, and a manservant, or at least a boy to help out. Larger homes of the gentry would have male servants and numerous indoor and outdoor servants.

There are simply too many domestic jobs for me to do justice to them all in this book; I'd have to write an encyclopedia! It's also hard to compare the various servants; a kitchen maid has very little in common with a lady's maid. I've narrowed these next chapters down to the more common positions that will probably crop up in your own manuscripts (and if they don't yet, you'll learn how to include them!).

## Upstairs, Downstairs, Middlestairs

Ok, I made up the middlestairs thing. I've made a bit of a gamble and I'm going to assume that most of you know the terms *upper servants* and *lower servants* from *Downton Abbey*. Since there were some changes in servants during the Georgian and Victorian age, I want to just give a quick history primer on servants.

Sadly, since The Dowager is from the Edwardian era, her grand wisdom is outside of this book's focus. But we shall sally forth! Or some such.

By the 17th century, the old system of servants that carried over from medieval times had pretty much disappeared. However, the hierarchy of servants remained and there was quite a firm and distinct division.

The upper servants were the more skilled and responsible servants. These were the stewards, butlers, housekeepers, male chefs (especially if he were French), tutors, and the like. The lower class servants, or the lower/downstairs crew, did the scrubbing, the kitchen work, laundry, and worked in the dairy.

Then, once the 18th century dawned, more specialized duties for servants were created or necessary to maintain both the giant estates and the smaller, more modest middle-class home. By then, the upper servants were cemented as the steward, housekeeper, personal maids, and valets, with the behind-closed-doors workers being put into the lower rank of servants.

The 19th century was what historian Jeremy Musson called the "apogee of domestic service", as the middle-class got wealthier and wealthier, requiring more and more servants[5].

I've tried to pick out jobs that were common across the 180-

odd years that this book covers. As ever, remember to double check the history of your specific servants if you aren't sure who did what and when!

# Women's Work

Domestic service wasn't just divided down job lines, but also gender. Women were paid less than men across the board. It wasn't until the late 17th century that female domestic staff began to outnumber the males in the house.

One of the most coveted positions in a wealthy household was that of **housekeeper**. The housekeeper was responsible for household affairs and the female servants and, according to Mrs. Beeton, the "immediate representative of her mistress."

**Our Experts**

Mrs. Radcliffe (*The Housekeeper's Guide*, 1823), Mrs. Beeton (*The Book of Household Management*, 1861), and Mr. Walsh (*A Manual of Domestic Economy*, 1856) wrote extensively about household management. You'll find their helpful, modern, and meticulous guidance essential to being a perfect servant.

The housekeeper was typically an older woman experienced in either running her own house or having been a domestic servant for a long time. She'd also need a firm grasp of basic accounting and money matters, since she would keep track of all the expenses she personally oversaw for the household. She'd be in charge of sending servants out to market, hiring tradesmen for various tasks, and purchasing various wares. All of those purchases would need to be entered into the ledgers for the steward or master of the house to inspect.

She was also in direct charge of the day-to-day minutia and nothing was too small to be beneath her notice. A keen eye was needed in a housekeeper, who would inspect linens for cleanliness, furniture for polish, and that hired tradesmen were doing their jobs. She might even operate as a tour guide for respectable tourists, such as Mrs. Reynolds in *Pride and Prejudice.*

Mrs. Radcliffe recommends that a housekeeper be a "grave, sober woman" because younger servants would respect her more

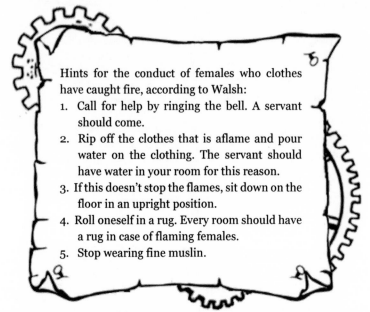

Hints for the conduct of females who clothes have caught fire, according to Walsh:

1. Call for help by ringing the bell. A servant should come.
2. Rip off the clothes that is aflame and pour water on the clothing. The servant should have water in your room for this reason.
3. If this doesn't stop the flames, sit down on the floor in an upright position.
4. Roll oneself in a rug. Every room should have a rug in case of flaming females.
5. Stop wearing fine muslin.

than if she were a "giddy, thoughtless person."

Another highly respectable position was the **lady's maid**, who could not be some slouch from the streets. The talents of a lady's maid were vast. She had to be literate and know needle-work. She should possess hairdressing skills, sewing and milliner skills, and understand the "art of perfumery[6]."

The lady's maid would lay out her mistress's clothing in the morning. Mud on the hems needed to be cleaned, and tweed and wool garments needed to be brushed. Any wrinkled muslin dresses from the previous day's wear required ironing if the lady wished to wear the dress again that day. Any small repairs also needed to be done. Boots needed cleaning and polishing.

The lady's maid was responsible for dressing her mistress and doing her hair. Curl-papers needed removing and if the 80s punk rock style was needed, the lady's maid needed to brush out those curls into a mess of fizzy hair:

> If bandeaux (fabric headband) are worn, the hair is thoroughly brushed and frizzed outside and inside, folding the hair back round the head, brushing it perfectly smooth, giving it a glossy appearance by the use of pomades, or oil, applied by the palm of the hand, smoothing it down with a small brush dipped in bandoline (similar to pomade)[7].

In fact, the lady's maid might be called upon to attend hairdressing classes to ensure she's up-to-date on all of the fashions.

She'd be in charge of cleaning brushes and combs, and keeping them well-repaired. She also might be required to wash laces and special muslins, and clean gold and silver items that were placed in the maid's care.

The lady's maid would travel with her mistress, packing the trunks, and ensuring her lady's comfort. And, for pity's sake, she should not be a gossip!

Martha is a lady's maid, though she works for an upper middle-class widow and not an aristocratic lady. Most middle class women didn't take on lady's maids because they either couldn't afford one or didn't have any use for one. However, many had an eye on the upper class and were happy to copy their ways. Also, widows living alone with grown children might find life rather dull without a young thing to keep her company.

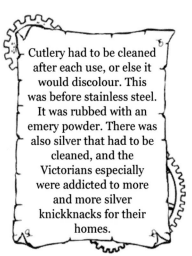

Cutlery had to be cleaned after each use, or else it would discolour. This was before stainless steel. It was rubbed with an emery powder. There was also silver that had to be cleaned, and the Victorians especially were addicted to more and more silver knickknacks for their homes.

Because of the smaller household, Martha might be sometimes called upon to assist the housemaids. Though her primary job would remain helping and entertaining her widowed mistress.

The **housemaid** was responsible for a clean house. In larger houses, housemaids might have assistants, the upper and under maids, and the work be divided between them.

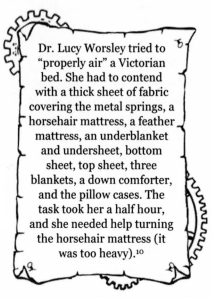

Dr. Lucy Worsley tried to "properly air" a Victorian bed. She had to contend with a thick sheet of fabric covering the metal springs, a horsehair mattress, a feather mattress, an underblanket and undersheet, bottom sheet, top sheet, three blankets, a down comforter, and the pillow cases. The task took her a half hour, and she needed help turning the horsehair mattress (it was too heavy).[10]

Housemaids were responsible for airing out rooms, sweeping up ashes, polishing the furniture, dusting everything daily, lighting fires, sweeping carpets, and beating rugs.

Upstairs, the bedrooms need airing, the beds changed and scrubbed down (to prevent bed bugs), the chamber pots emptied, beds made, chairs brushed, floors swept, and basins cleaned.

Tired yet?

Don't worry, because once the cleaning is done, there is still mealtimes and helping serve meals. Then dishes have to be done and table linens all need ironing and folding. Tables need scrubbing and knives arranging.

In the housemaid's spare time, "the housemaid should be able to do some needlework[8]" such as mending sheets and darning linens.

Of course, the house will need to occasionally have a great big ol' scrubbing top to bottom, where every piece of furniture is moved, the walls washed, the floors scrubbed, mattresses beaten, and "thoroughly purifying every article of furniture[9]" before putting it back.

Whew. I need a nap.

The **governess** wasn't a family member and wasn't a servant; she was neither and, because of that, outcast in every social circle excepting her own. In 1850, there were 21,000 registered governesses in the country, and "probably many of them were well-educated but impoverished.[11]"

For generations, privileged daughters were educated at home by governesses. These women of education, but without fortune, often taught both the boys and the girls in the house. The boys might go on to school or even university, and the governess might stay on to teach the young ladies how to be refined and accomplished women.

Literature from the period is full of governesses and them getting lives they deserve. Miss Taylor (*Emma*) has a wonderful position with the Woodhouses until a wealthy, decent man sweeps her off her feet. Jane Fairfax (*Emma*) likewise falls in love with a rich heir and marries without needing to actually degrade herself to have to earn her way in life. Diana and Mary Rivers (*Jane Eyre*) went to school knowing they would need to become governesses because their father had lost their inheritance.

> For middle-class families, girls could attend school. Early girls' schools focused on female accomplishments such as the piano, drawing, foreign languages, and needlework. It wasn't until the 1860s that curriculum began to match what boys were taught.[12]

And perhaps the most famous governess, Jane Eyre herself. Abused, neglected, forgotten, not only made her own way in the world, but became an heiress in her own right. She rescued Diana and Mary Rivers by giving them some of her inheritance, and went on to marry the gentleman of her dreams, Mr. Rochester, who liked to lock women in the attic.

One of the reasons the governess was so heavily featured was that she was pitied by many. If it hadn't been for her wealthy brothers, Jane Austen herself would have most likely ended up a governess. Governesses like Nelly Weeton, a prolific diarist from Northern England, were intelligent and educated, but were considered low-class because they were governesses. In 1812, Weeton moved to Yorkshire and wrote this about her life as a governess:

> A governess is almost shut out of society; not choosing to associate with servants, and not being treated as an equal by the heads of the house or their visitors, she must possess some fortitude and strength of mind to render herself tranquil or happy; but indeed, the master or mistress of a house, if they have any goodness of heart, would take pains to prevent her feeling her inferiority. For my own part, I have no cause of just complaint; but I know some that are treated in a most mortifying manner[13].

In *Advice to Governesses*, the anonymous author gives practical life advice for the young, pretty governess. Basically, stay as far away from the boys as possible and, for goodness sake, don't fantasize about marrying any rich, handsome man who comes to visit: "Let her not for a moment indulge the thought that a marriage with any of them may be contracted with impunity because such marriages have been made."

I wonder if Mrs. Fairfax in *Jane Eyre* had read the same book when she told Jane, "Gentlemen in his station are not accustomed to marry their governesses."

Words to live by. Make sure the sensible friend in your novel says this often to your governess heroine whenever she's eyeing the tasty master of the house.

Another popular job was the nurse. The role of nurse can cover a number of different positions, though perhaps the most common is that of the **wet nurse** and the **nursery-maid**. They might be two different nurses, or the same woman. There were also women who took in children to care for them in their homes, similar to a modern daycare.

The nursery-maid was in charge of the children. As the primary caretaker of all of the little heirs and heiresses, her role was vital to the survival of England's rake population. Her job was to use modern medical practices, such as never bathing a child with a full stomach. Nor allowing children outside with wet hair, as they will most likely die. Oh, and bathing should be accompanied with lively singing to avoid depressed spirits.

Good nursery-maids were to ensure that no spice nor wine was added to their food. They should only eat food the temperature of breast milk. To do otherwise, the nursery-maid risked filling a child's stomach with slime.

Slime is no laughing matter.

The nursery-maid must resist giving teething children glass to chew on, and instead give them biscuits and bread crusts. (What sober person would give *glass* to a baby to chew on?)

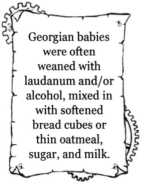

Georgian babies were often weaned with laudanum and/or alcohol, mixed in with softened bread cubes or thin oatmeal, sugar, and milk.

Don't feed children at night; it makes them fat and bloated. Never give them tea; it kills children. And, for pity's sake, don't give children opioids to make them sleep. Sigh. This is perhaps the hardest job of all.

In the modern world, women are encouraged to breastfeed their newborns. In earlier times, women of means often didn't breastfeed their own children. There were a number of reasons for that, but one common reason was being forbidden by the husband. A woman who'd given birth to a girl would be expected to return to the marital bed as soon as possible in hopes of producing a male heir[14]. Exclusive breastfeeding could interfere with conception and a lady needed to pop out an heir and a spare before she could go sleep with someone she actually liked.

However, wet nurses weren't always the most responsible. Some were alcoholics and newborns were neglected and sometimes even crushed by a nurse after she'd passed out on top of them. This wasn't a problem only affecting the lower-classes; the famous Georgiana, Duchess of Devonshire ended up breastfeeding her own daughter after discovering the infant's nurse was often drunk[15].

By the 1860s, bottle-feeding became popular and cheaply available, which became a safer means for nurses to feed infants and wet-nurses declined in popularity[16].

# Manly Man Jobs

If the housekeeper was the mistress of the servants, than the **steward** was the master. The steward had to be educated and good with accounts, as his job entailed household management, administration, and accounting. In the early part of the 18th century, the steward might also look after the estate's workers, tenants, and rentals.

By the 19th century, the steward, housekeeper, and butler worked in tandem whenever important guests were to arrive. The steward also helped in hiring, managing, and firing servants as required, paid household bills, and looked after the servant's wages[17].

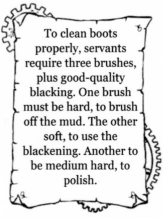

To clean boots properly, servants require three brushes, plus good-quality blacking. One brush must be hard, to brush off the mud. The other soft, to use the blackening. Another to be medium hard, to polish.

This wasn't a lowly job, either. Stewards in the very wealthy homes, with 30-50 servants, would have made up to £1000 per year in the early 18th century!

The **butler** was the male counterpart of the housekeeper. If there isn't someone else to do the job, the butler began his day at 6am cleaning boots, shoes, and knives. It was his job to have the table set for breakfast and to wait on the family during the meal, though he might be assisted by a footman. He cleared away the dishes and cleaned the table. He was also in charge of serving luncheon unassisted. Again, he assisted with dinner, ringing the bell after the end of each course, handing dishes to servants. Rinse and repeat for the other courses.

In between meals, the butler would also answer the bell. He'd also check lamps, candles, and (later) gas burners to ensure all were working and safe.

In houses with only a footman, the butler may also do some of the duties of a valet, including paying bills and serving as a valet when required.

All of the fancy plates were locked up under his care, and at night he was responsible for locking the doors and windows, and ensuring all of the fires are safe. He'd be in charge of the wine cellar and keep excellent records of the contents.

Trust is paramount when hiring a butler.[18]

The **footman** might be one of many or just himself. His entire job description can be summarized as "be useful." The footman must rise early to get dirty work done before the family gets up, especially the cleaning of a lady's boots. "Much delicacy" must be taken in cleaning a lady's boots, as hand-marks on the leather are "very offensive" to a lady of refined tastes.

Silk hats require daily brushing. After rain, it should be wiped down, nearly dried, than brushed down.

He'd also help clean the knives, furniture, and plates, attend the bell, and do errands as required by the butler or housekeeper. In a house without a valet, the footman would take over some of those tasks, such as brushing down clothes of the master.

The footman might be in charge of delivering the tea tray. Or that the carriage was clean and "free from dust." Also, he should make sure that the lady's dress isn't caught in the door. The footman might also carry messages or letters to the post, friends, or to tradespeople[19].

The **valet** was similar to the lady's maid or waiting maid, only he served the master. He dressed them, and accompanied them on all journeys. "Good sense, some self-denial, and consideration for the feelings of others" are all good skills for a valet to have.

The valet started his day by making sure the dressing room was in order, that the housemaid had already swept and dusted it, that the fire was burning safely. The valet would air out the room, but ensure that it returned to the temperature his master preferred before his master awoke. Body linen was warmed and aired by the fire, trousers were laid out and brushed and cleaned, and the coast and waistcoat was brushed and folded, ready for use. Razors were set up and hot water ready for use.

He should be a good hairdresser and able to shave his master, if that's his preference. He should cut the master's hair every 2-3 weeks and trim whiskers as needed.

The valet would hand his master his cane, gloves, and hat. Then he cleaned up the dressing room.

The valet was in charge of keeping items cleaned. The cravat that wasn't changed every day should be ironed to get rid of creases. Grease spots on coat collars should be cleaned. Daily. Boots should be polished.

He might be called upon to convey messages to friends or tradesmen and ensure that his master's bed clothes were ready for the evening before bed[20].

## It's Pay Day!

In Medieval and Tudor times, men dominated domestic service. Even the kitchens were full of men and boys. This began to change in the late seventeenth century when females took over. Even housekeepers took on important roles within the household. Cleaning, cooking, and laundry became women's chores—something that has not changed since[21]. Female workers were paid less than male workers, and domestic service was included in that inequality.

The housemaid was paid around £5 per year in the late 1700s. If she was pretty and young, she could make £2 for a night of sex. In the mid-Victorian period, a maid-of-all-work who lived at the house made about £6 a year, while a general domestic servant made £16. Compare that with the £42 a live-in manservant made. And compare all that with the £25 per half hour a top prostitute charged.

Seeing a trend yet? It's little wonder why so many young, poor women turned to prostitution. A life of supposed glamour (and, indeed, it sometimes was) or a life of drudgery.

When Walsh published his book in 1856, a housemaid made £10-£16, cooks made £10-£24, and maids-of-all-work varied around £4-£10. This sometimes included tea, sugar, and washing. If not, they could expect to be paid an additional two guineas for tea and sugar, and one guinea for washing.

Some servants got "vails" or tips. It's why Becky Sharp's trunks weren't handed down to her in *Vanity Fair* (1843); she didn't have money to tip, so why bother? Mid-Victorian female guests might tip household maids five shillings for a long weekend stay and ten shillings for a week. Gentlemen would tip the house valet if they didn't bring their own, and might give the coachman a half crown if he drove him around. Of course, this didn't mean that everyone did it or tipped that much![22]

Family might tip or give bonuses, too, especially at Christmas. First, perhaps the servants would be permitted to sleep in to eight or even nine in the morning. They might be served a meal like William Tyler's rich widow employer served one year: roast beef, plum pudding, turkey, and a bottle of brandy for the servants to make punch with. The old lady's son-in-law gave Tyler a sovereign coin (£1) because he was a frequent visitor and often required Tyler's assistance[23].

Would your hero tip well to impress the ladies, or would he be stingy? Your heroine's good opinion might be lost forever if he treated her servants poorly.

A great way for your protagonist to show that he cares about his servants is to send for a doctor for them when they are ill. A master who fetches a doctor for a servant must pay for the fees and cannot deduct the fee from the servant's wages in the 1850s. By fetching the doctor himself, he takes on the financial responsibilities like a good employer should[24].

Speaking in general terms, there were some expectations of the employee-employer relationship. Servants could expect a couple weeks of vacation every year to visit their family, provided they had permission and the funds to travel. Many could expect a half day off on Sunday to attend church, an evening out once per week, and a day off every month.

In the 1850s, for example, a month's notice was required to leave one's employment, unless a contract pre-arranged different terms. If the servant was discharged without notice, they were paid one month's salary. If a female servant got married and didn't provide her notice, she still had to finish working her month and not even her husband could take her away[25].

As with modern companies, some people get less than what's legal, some get the base amount, and others get well beyond the average. Rules and guidelines for terminating servants changed over time, so double check the law and common practice for your book's time period.

## Hannah Cullwick (1833-1909)

was a mid-Victorian maid and a prolific diarist. She is perhaps best known for what we'd today call a form of BDSM relationship called "Dominance and Submission." Hannah had a life-long relationship with Arthur Munby, an upper class lawyer, whom she eventually married in secret and often lived apart from for various health and personal reasons.

But while known for her sexual relationship with Munby, she provided modern readers a rare look inside the day-to-day life of a maid-of-all-work. Through her, we can see inside the life of one of the lower status domestic servants.

When Hannah was 14 years of age, she was hired to look after eight . . . count them . . . eight children. She was paid 2s a week (£6/year). She was in charge of washing and dressing each of them by 8am. She also cleaned the children's footwear, scrubbed their nurseries, the hallway outside, and the stairs leading up to the hallway (leading to the nurseries). She also was in charge of getting the children's meals, bringing water up for baths, coals for the fire, and putting the kids in bed. They wouldn't allow her to travel to her parents' funerals because she might bring back infection.

As a young adult, she worked as a general servant for a while and made £16 a year, significantly more than as a teenager. She did typical general domestic chores, plus cleaned knives and boots, and the outside doorstep. At another job, she cleaned five fireplaces, plus was in charge of cleaning the dining room, study, hallways, outdoor steps, lady's maid's room, and the lower ground floor[1].

She commented at the end of 1860 that she had cleaned 927 pairs of boots that year.

# Chapter 7: Below Decks

*"The maid of all work is generally supposed to live on little more than the leavings of the table."*
-John Henry Walsh, *A Manual of Domestic Economy*

If we treat Georgian and Victorian estates like businesses, then the upper servants in the previous chapter were all of the management, directors, and executives. Outside of the owners themselves, they were the voice of the house who managed themselves and others. That leaves everyone else in the house to be the peons who work late, arrive early, and who are expected to eat their lunch in front of a computer screen.

Welcome to the world of the lower servants.

## A Woman's Place

With the medieval times well behind England, the cheap rates of women were embraced. It was no longer seen in a negative way to have women working in one's kitchens and laundry rooms. That meant that everyone had female staff by the early Georgian period.

In the last chapter, we discussed Mrs. Beeton's opinions on what middle class families should have for domestic servants. There were female positions recommended for all levels of the middle-class.

There's one slight asterisk on the role of housemaid from last chapter. In very large houses, the role of housemaid might be split into two different jobs: upper housemaid and **under (or lower) housemaid**. In this case, the under housemaids would be under the upper housemaids and would have to assist them, as needed. Mrs. Beeton notes that the upper housemaids would focus on furniture and assisting the family, leaving the dirty work for the under housemaids.

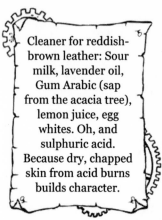

Cleaner for reddish-brown leather: Sour milk, lavender oil, Gum Arabic (sap from the acacia tree), lemon juice, egg whites. Oh, and sulphuric acid. Because dry, chapped skin from acid burns builds character.

Anyone with children knows how much laundry they generate simply by being kids. Even in an era where refined girls weren't allowed to play in the mud with her brothers, she would still have jam all down the front of her smock and mashed potatoes in her hair. Likewise, without deodorant, the teenagers of the house would have smelled like rotting potatoes in the summer months.

Plus, the linens, underclothing, rags, and all of the usual laundry needs of a household would need to be eventually washed. Comfortably middle-class homes could afford to hire a **laundry-maid** to look after the washing.

Mrs. Radcliffe says that these women were usually raised to be these, but any young woman can be trained since "all women are more or less acquainted with washing." Laundry-maids needed to be regular with their wash days, and needed to keep their wash tubs clean. She'd also need to separate clothes and stain treat them. Laundry "day" was actually several days!

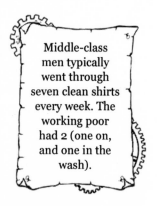

Middle-class men typically went through seven clean shirts every week. The working poor had 2 (one on, and one in the wash).

Laundry was a massive undertaking. Good fire, boiling water, cauldrons and coppers, irons, soap, and starch, plus the woman-hours involved. In the BBC production of *Victorian Farm*, historian Ruth Goodman reproduces a typical wash day in the Victorian age. It's quite eye-opening!

She spent Saturday sorting her laundry by fabric and colour. All mending needed to be done first, as well as stain treating, before being soaked overnight. She started washing Sunday morning at 4 am and spent all day scrubbing, rinsing, and wringing clothes.

An in-house laundry-maid would also be responsible for ironing and starching clothing. It took Goodman two days for those tasks. Tuesday was starching day, where all of the clothes had to be dipped into starch and hung to dry. She spent Wednesday ironing clothes and putting them away. Laundry "day" was actually half a week!

Down in the kitchen, the **cook** would be running a tight food factory. Grand houses might have a male French chef, but most homes had a female running the kitchen. The cook should be a neat and clean lady, careful in her work, and aware of what was happening in her kitchen at all times. She had to be trustworthy, as she was entrusted with salt, sugar, spices, and meat. Giving away any of those precious supplies without approval was theft and grounds for immediate dismissal.

For a detailed wash description, I recommend "The Laundry Timetable" in *Victorian Farm* by Alex Langlands, Peter Ginn, and Ruth Goodman.

The cook generally arranged meals as she saw fit, though the mistress might take it upon herself to provide recommendations, especially in the case of company. After the kitchen fires were lit, the cook started breakfast. After breakfast, she'd need to go to market, or arrange for an assistant to go. She'd be required to work on dinner and luncheon at the same time, as well as prepare something for tea time. The washing of the cooking dishes fell under her care.

In smaller homes, the cook might help the housemaid with making the beds; it was typically a two-person task. If there wasn't a man assigned to the task, she'd also clean the cutlery after every meal and help out with cleaning boots and shoes.

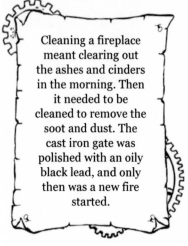

Cleaning a fireplace meant clearing out the ashes and cinders in the morning. Then it needed to be cleaned to remove the soot and dust. The cast iron gate was polished with an oily black lead, and only then was a new fire started.

Cooks might also be called upon to make extra food for distribution to the poor. Mrs. Rundell recommends a "gratuity at the end of the winter" for any cook that is "one of those rare creatures" who require a reward for the extra work.

The **kitchen-maid** assisted the cook. The kitchen-maid was often in charge of lighting the kitchen fire or stove, plus keeping the kitchen swept and clean. She'd also be in charge of the area outside of the kitchen, such as the hallways and stairs, and tasked with cleaning food storage tables, shelves, and cupboards twice a week.

She ensured dishes were put away, and that the copper and brass cookware were properly looked after. This was a health and safety issue, as there was a risk of the tinning coming off and poisoning people. Then again, maybe your kitchen-maid just couldn't care less.

When her work was done for the day, she needed to assist other servants, be clean, and never "dress above her station."

The poor **scullery-maid** assisted the cook and kept the scullery clean, and was often in charge of cleaning all kitchen utensils. She was poorly paid and treated even worse, and was often very young. If she was very lucky, she might pick up some cooking knowledge that could serve her later in life and help secure a new, better paying position.

The **maid-of-all-work** had a pitiable plight, as her work, according to Mrs. Beeton, was "never done." Walsh called her the servant of "general drudge." In a house with no other housemaid, the maid-of-all-work was expected to do all of the work that was needed to clean and upkeep a house, all without "destroying her own health."

Maids-of-all-work often risked being treated worse than other servants. These maids were typically around thirteen years of age or thereabouts; a prime age for abuse, neglect, and lacking the skills to find a better situation.

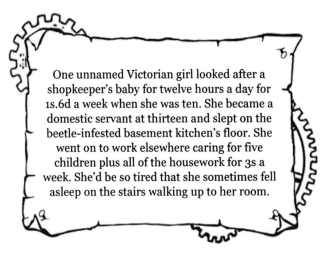

One unnamed Victorian girl looked after a shopkeeper's baby for twelve hours a day for 1s.6d a week when she was ten. She became a domestic servant at thirteen and slept on the beetle-infested basement kitchen's floor. She went on to work elsewhere caring for five children plus all of the housework for 3s a week. She'd be so tired that she sometimes fell asleep on the stairs walking up to her room.

## He's Just the Son of Mr. Darcy's Steward

The **coachman**, you might guess, dealt with the coach and horses. The coachman would be in charge of the groom and stable-boy. He needed a firm knowledge of horses. He watched over them and ensured they were properly fed. He'd be responsible for applying home remedies to small ailments and reporting the serious ones beyond his skill. Either he or the stable boy was in charge of cleaning the carriage.

I wasn't quite sure where to put the **groom**, as his position would vary depending upon the size of the house. The groom kept the horses in good condition, but might occasionally fill in for a valet, such as riding out with his master, waiting at table, or otherwise assist within the house itself. The groom and stable boy also ensured the stables were clean and the horses exercised and watered.

Some houses might have a **stable boy**. A stable-boy would

clean the carriage, but also be in charge of the stables themselves. That means removing horse dung, plus sweeping and washing the stables. He'd be responsible for this every day.

The **footboy** was a young boy who got his start cleaning boots and carrying luggage. While his salary was abysmal, his job came with the possibility of tips from visiting guests, which helped supplement his income. He might light some of the fires, clean boots belonging to the upper servants, clean windows and mirrors, and help carry boxes and luggage into the house for guests[2].

# The Scourge of Servants: Company

I started Chapter 6 talking about parties, so I wanted to explore how servants were affected by having, let's say, twenty people over for supper. There might be an impromptu dance afterward and, if the weather turns poorly, perhaps our guests might spend the night, provided genteel accommodations could be made for them.

After all, the goal is to marry off the rakes, not give them fresh-faced victims.

First, an upper-class mistress would sit down with her housekeeper and work out the menu. The housekeeper would have a keen knowledge for what would be available at the market and what was in the storerooms.

After some discussion, the housekeeper

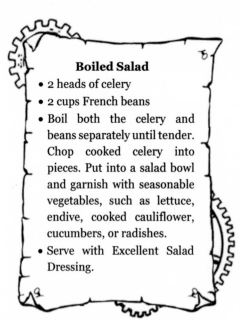

**Boiled Salad**
- 2 heads of celery
- 2 cups French beans
- Boil both the celery and beans separately until tender. Chop cooked celery into pieces. Put into a salad bowl and garnish with seasonable vegetables, such as lettuce, endive, cooked cauliflower, cucumbers, or radishes.
- Serve with Excellent Salad Dressing.

convinces her mistress that smoked fish and roasted pork would be perfect ways to impress their dinner guests. The mistress insists on turtle soup, and the housekeeper recommends that boiled mutton and a goose pie would really help round out the meal.

With the heavy dishes taken care of, the housekeeper suggests stewed cabbage and a gooseberry tart made with preserves from the pantry. The master of the house loves boiled salad, so that is added to the menu.

No meal can exist without sauces and gravies, so the housekeeper recommends pork gravy, oiled butter, shallot sauce, and some walnut ketchup for the roasted pork.

Our Regency heroine, Martha, might have had started out a scullery or kitchen maid as a youngster. On party nights back then, she'd have easily been faced with *five hundred or more* dishes. There were no rubber gloves back then, so her hands would be in hot water for hours upon hours trying to scrape the burnt-on bits and the grease off the pots and pans.

It seems like an over-exaggeration; surely not that many articles would be dirtied. But, consider what goes into a big feast. I normally put on a large feast every year at my house. In 2012, I served a medieval country aristocratic-themed dinner. The menu was a hand-smoked pork that was slow-roasted, boiled cabbage and carrots, turnip potage, cheesecakes, fritters, homemade sausages, pies, a boiled salad, salt beef, and a host of other dishes. It took over two hours to serve the meal.

The feast generated over a thousand dirty dishes by the end. And I live in the modern world, with a microwave, indoor plumbing, and a dishwasher! It would be significantly worse for Martha, who would be faced with pots made of iron, copper, and brass, all having burnt food stuck to them. Kettles would be covered in soot. Frying pans, roasting irons, and roasting pans will all be covered with crusted skin and pig fat. Towels, cheesecloth, and serving mitts will need to be rinsed out for the laundry. Serving platters, gravy boats, and plates will all need to be emptied and cleaned. The small things like mills, mortar and pestles, and the like will all need to be cleaned and put away.

Let's not forget all of the glasses, plates, bowls, spoons, knives, forks, and napkins from the meal itself! It's a lot of work and all of those need to be cleaned without a dishwasher and stainless steel.

**Excellent Salad Dressing**
Mix 1 tsp mustard with 1 tsp of sugar in a bowl. Slowly drizzle 2 tbsp olive oil into the mixture, carefully stirring until smooth. Add 2 tbsp of vinegar and 4 tbsp of milk the same way to ensure the dressing doesn't curdle. Add salt and crushed red peppers to taste. Chef's note: "The ingredients cannot be added too gradually, or stirred too much[3]."

So while Martha is busy scrubbing the dishes as the meal is being prepared, maids and footmen are running around fetching groceries from the costermongers, butcher, fishmonger, and grocery. Maids were busy ironing linens and butlers were busy scrubbing down the dining table.

In the days leading up to the party, maids repaired dresses. Gloves were purchased. Shoes cleaned. Parasols fetched. Hats trimmed. Sideburns trimmed. Boots buffed. Jackets brushed.

Coachmen and footmen prepared the barouche-box and transported their guests. If it were cold outside, lambskins or blankets would be tossed over ladies' laps to ward off pneumonia and death.

Footmen would be needed to serve the meal itself, along with the butler's help, and the kitchen staff would be frantically getting each dish ready to go. House maids would be scurrying around cleaning up slopped food in the corridors.

But what happens if the weather turns too nasty to drive home? Slumber party! Well, not for the servants, but who cares about them in any case.

Hot water would need to be fetched for all of the overnight

guests, so that they could wash. Fires would be lit in every bedchamber.

In the morning, their boots would be cleaned, their fires re-lit, if necessary, and curtains opened (the wealthy have never been trained on how to properly open a curtain). More hot water, more maids cleaning chamber pots, and even more cooking needed to take place . . . because breakfast had to be served.

Domestic work never ends.

## Scrubbing Floors and More

No book by me would be complete without me trying out some of the advice handed out by period experts. Sadly for all of you, I do not have any tales of ruining the drywall, bathing my dog in lard, and having mushrooms marinated in cat pee. For those of you who are new to my books, it's okay if you're staring at this paragraph in confused horror. Those of you who read the first book are probably all moaning in disappointment; I know how much you loved me ruining my walls!

I spent two days working as a maid-of-all-work in my own home. It was horrible. I thought I worked hard before, but it was even worse trying to keep up with the expectations of Mrs. Beeton and company. I didn't give up all modern conveniences, because even I draw a line in the sand. Last book, it was at soaking a dead chicken in beer. This time around it was giving up electricity and plumbing.

*5am: Isn't there a law against getting up this early? I'm a writer; I sleep late.*

I crawled out of bed in the dark, dressed myself, and headed to the fireplace. First things first: the fire. In the pre-electricity and gas world, the fires needed to be lit first for heat, water, and food. I grew up with a wood furnace, so I'm an expert firebug. Unfortunately, the fireplace would need to be scrubbed first. Victorian ranges needed to be cleaned and blackened every morning, but I was working with an open fireplace. I settled for removing the ash and old wood, and then giving it a thorough scrub.

I use my fireplace frequently, but I'd never scrubbed it before. Wooden brush and pail of water in hand, I scrubbed that puppy until it sparkled. My knees ached, my back hurt, and my right shoulder felt like it was going to fall off. But after *forty-five minutes* of cleaning, I was ready to light the fire.

With the fire now going, I could turn my attention to hot water for the master of the house (let's hope he's enjoying this because he'll never be called that ever again!). I put water on to boil while settling in to make breakfast. I put out cold pork, cut fruit, cheese, and bread. I filled up the sinks of the house with the pot of boiling water, which was a lot of effort. I burned two fingers on the pot, another on the water itself, and had small red spots all over my hands from where the water splashed up.

*8am: Chamber pots and more*

I got to eat my own breakfast once the kids had polished off the food, leaving me a piece of pork gristle and the bruised half of an apple. Thanks, boys; you're so grounded. I had 6 ounces of bread with butter, which is about 3 sandwich buns. It was a lot of bread and I felt bloated, but it was pretty much what got me through the day.

I got a beer allowance, but my old lady stomach can't handle liquor that early in the morning! I made myself tea and totally stole sugar and cream, even though I didn't get a sugar allowance with my wages. I saved the beer for later in the day.

It was time to get started on cleaning. I scrubbed up the breakfast dishes, using hot water from a pot on the stove. With my trusty brush, rag bag, and my bucket of hot water, I went to work scrubbing the toilets and bathtub by hand.

The bedrooms needed to be aired out. I have teenagers, so that was a task not for the faint of heart. I flipped the mattresses for the kids' beds, but wasn't strong enough to flip my king-size mattress alone. I scrubbed the bedframes down in an attempt to ward off bedbugs, and made the beds, after shaking out the blankets. I closed the windows and made a note to ground the kids for having disgusting rooms.

I outsourced the laundry to our part-time laundry-maid, *Maytag*. I cleaned all of the footwear in the house. It kills me to admit this, but I really do have too many shoes. The outdoor steps probably needed to be cleaned, since I've never actually cleaned them. Upon inspection, I discovered they were absolutely gross. What would Mrs. Beeton have said if she'd seen the state of those steps? I'm surprised I hadn't lost my position yet.

I got to work scrubbing the concrete slab and the steps up to the door. Then I realized, to my horror, that wild rabbits had pooped on my deck and a horde of cats had been peeing next to the door. So back on my hands and knees and more scrubbing.

It wasn't even noon and I was ready to burn the house down and collect the insurance money.

*11am: When is nap time?*

The master (heavens, I can't type that without laughing) likes to eat his meals later than most, so I started working on both luncheon and dinner. By now, my hands were raw from all of the hot water and scrubbing, and my back was screaming in agony.

**To blacken the fronts of stone chimney-pieces:** Mix oil-varnish with lamp-black, and a little turpentine to thin it. Wash the stone with soap and water first, then sponge it with clear water. When dry, brush it over twice with mixture, letting it dry completely between applications[4].

My apron was filthy, as was the hem of my dress. And the sleeves up to the elbows were wet and grimy. Thankfully, I was wearing a sturdy, but unfashionable dress that I'd quick-sewn in an afternoon. I know myself; I'm a messy cleaner.

Did I mention that I was doing all of this in a corset? That's right, a corset. At this juncture, the argument begins over if corsets are painful. After all, properly-fitting corsets shouldn't hurt and so on. It's 100% true; a custom corset to your body isn't going to nip, pull, crush, or torture you without your consent. And your back is going to ache if you aren't used to working in one. I'm not used to wearing one, so my back muscles were so angry that I'd need more than a couple beers and a massage by the time this was over.

Since the children wouldn't be at home for luncheon and dinner today, I laid out a simple meal of soup, salad, and bread toasted by the fire, just the way the master (*snort*) likes it.

*1pm: I demand a raise.*

I was able to take a few minutes to eat another 6 ounces of bread with butter, a slice of cheese, and a light beer. I didn't have time for anything else. There was too much to do. All of the cutlery used thus far had to be polished, else it would turn colour. Of course, I use stainless steel, but I dutifully polished all of the knives and cutlery used so far in the day. The furniture needed to be dusted and the animals brushed. I washed the dog, though I let the cats bathe themselves. I did brush them all, though.

I also swept and scrubbed the floors on my hands and knees. I have a 1300 square foot house and it never felt so freaking massive. Why didn't we live in a hut?

Oh, and I was still cooking dinner throughout all this!

*6pm: Seriously, I need a raise. And a beer. And maybe some morphine.*

By now, my knees were wobbly from having been knelt on all day. Every muscle in my back had fused into a giant knot. My hands were cracked and angry-red. I had paper cuts, burst blisters, hangnails that had bled, and I'd torn two nails below the quick. Oh, and I couldn't look over my right shoulder anymore.

As the children of the household were elsewhere (thank you for small mercies), I laid out a simple family meal, based on Mrs. Beeton's suggestions. Leftover chicken fricasseed, roasted pork with chutney sauce, Brussels sprouts and bacon, and lemon pie.

Simple meal my sore ass.

*7pm: Does every sock have a hole in it?*

The dinner dishes were finally all done, as well as the cutlery and knife polishing. I was able to have a bowl of soup left from lunch, along with a half a pound of bread, butter, some cheese, and two beers. There were a couple pieces of pork left, so I ate that, too. I was still hungry, but at least I didn't feel faint anymore.

*Maytag* miraculously delivered the laundry, sans ironing. I piled up all of the clothing in need of mending, which was nearly every stitch of clothes in the house. Seriously, did the kids pull buttons off their shirts on purpose for this?

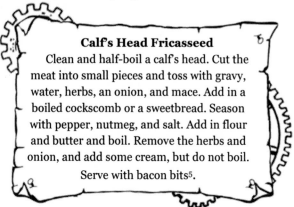

**Calf's Head Fricasseed**

Clean and half-boil a calf's head. Cut the meat into small pieces and toss with gravy, water, herbs, an onion, and mace. Add in a boiled cockscomb or a sweetbread. Season with pepper, nutmeg, and salt. Add in flour and butter and boil. Remove the herbs and onion, and add some cream, but do not boil. Serve with bacon bits[5].

I sat in front of the fire and darned socks, repaired pant hems, stitched holes, and reattached buttons. My eyesight isn't the best, and it was difficult seeing using nothing more than candlelight and the fireplace. My hands were shaky from all of the scrubbing and I had a piercing headache that made my vision blurry.

*9pm: Are you people really that dirty?*

More water in the sinks for washing up. Beds were turned down and space heaters turned on. Dirty clothes were picked up and put into baskets. Coats were hung up.

*10pm: Bedtime*

Zzzzzzzzz.

*5am: What fresh hell is this?*

It was nigh impossible to get out of bed. Every part of my body ached. My hands were swollen from all of the hot water, soaps, and scrubbing. I had random bruises over my body that I didn't remember earning, and my knees were swollen and bruised. My stomach was eating itself from hunger. My guts were protesting the pound of bread I'd eaten the day before, and I normally don't ever drink that much beer in one day, let alone when I'm working that hard. I didn't drink any water during the previous day (just tea and beer), so my tongue was practically sticking to the roof of my mouth. My lips were cracked and bled when I yawned.

I dragged myself out of bed and decided that, if I'd been born in the Regency, I'd have become a prostitute long before becoming a maid-of-all-work.

## Odds and Ends Pay the Bills

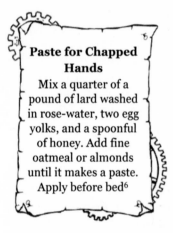

**Paste for Chapped Hands**

Mix a quarter of a pound of lard washed in rose-water, two egg yolks, and a spoonful of honey. Add fine oatmeal or almonds until it makes a paste. Apply before bed[6]

Not every servant got food and lodgings as part of the package. Many of the more casual, part-time, and temporary workers came in, did a job, and left. Mrs. Beeton's chart earlier said that a household making £100 a year could make do with a maid-of-all-work. What about the families who only made £30 a year, but needed help? That's where the casual work comes into play.

Some households, especially ones with larger, extended families living with them, could afford a couple of rooms and one with a stove or at least a small fireplace. The older women would stay at home to do sewing or mending, while a pregnant woman would be home sewing, mending, or ironing. A neighbour's twelve-year-old might be brought in to help with the toddlers who were underfoot while the women of the house did whatever paid work they could procure for the day or week. The twelve-year-old would be doing the work of a maid-of-all-work or a nurserymaid, but she'd only be needed a couple days a week, and wouldn't live at the house.

Small clerk offices and shops might bring a cleaner a couple times a week, or a few hours a day, to wipe down the furniture, clean the coal stove, scour the floors, and scrub the outside steps and windows.

Odd jobs were where children and young teenagers were useful. A twelve-year-old boy could chop firewood and load crates on wagons. Those were full-time, permanent placement jobs, but sometimes just special one-off jobs. A smart lad with connections would know when his skills were needed and, if he got a good reputation for hard work, might find a permanent placement.

## I Hate My Job

Reading mistresses' diaries and servants' diaries, I've come to the conclusion that complaining about one's job and one's employees is one of those universal things that spans humanity. Just like eating, sleeping, and sex, complaining about your horrible boss is ingrained in us.

Employers complained about their servants. Employees complained about their masters.

Many maids were teenager girls. I've been a teenage girl and, speaking from experience, I think some of the complaints about servants were probably warranted! A sixteen-year-old girl is a sixteen-year-old girl. Sometimes, there's no controlling her flirting, gossiping, and troublemaking, be it 1813 or 2013!

There is one interesting collection of letters, however, in a book called *Toilers of London*. They were several anonymous letters passed from servants through a pastor. There were letters by young women like "Hopeful" who'd been enticed to move to London to work. She worked at a house with twenty-nine people living there and only four of them were servants. At eighteen years of age, she wasn't allowed to go out in her free time. She worked from six in the morning to ten at night. "Masters and mistresses," she writes, "forget that servants are human beings like themselves."

A popular 1880s guide recommended servants only needed a bed and bedstead, sheets, a chest of drawers, a mirror, a washstand, and a chair.[7]

Sundays were busy days for servants. Despite their own personal beliefs, a servant could not refuse to work on Sunday. If she had time to go to church, or was forced, she should go, though a servant might find they did not have a say in what church or faith they attended. If she couldn't attend church, she should still find time to pray and read the Bible . . . oh, and make the fires and beds, dress the family, milk the cows, feed the pigs, dust the vases, and do anything else that was necessary around the house.

A common fear was losing one's position and not getting a character reference, thereby making a woman desperate and destitute. "You promised not to tell my name . . . because I might never get another place if my mistresses got ear I had been complaining," Anonymous wrote.

Crystal Palace thinks "ladies have not enough work themselves, and that is why they like to call us servants lazy." Her mistress likes to purposely knock over items and then make her maids clean up the mess.

Kensington writes that, "I've heard our coachman say his horses are better taken care of than us servants." Not surprising, since court records in house breaking cases from the Old Bailey showed that some servants slept in front of the doors to catch burglars.

Now, Mrs. Radcliffe believes servants should be treated fairly and kindly. From her perspective, a person earning a living in "an honest way" shouldn't be treated contemptuously. Of course, she always believed people should be "content with the station in which Providence" placed them.[8]

However, Mrs. Radcliffe was very stern in her views concerning dishonest servants, particularly those who engaged in the "market penny." A servant sent with cash to the market or in charge of paying tradesmen for whatever task they've performed might skim a bit off the top by adding a penny to the bill. Sorta like when you send your kid to 7-Eleven with a ten to pick up a bag of chips for you and you get a few coins and the smallest bag of chips ever created. While annoying to mistresses and mothers the world over, this is a great way for your own heroine to find some pocket money![9]

I know that I've painted a pretty bleak picture of the daily lives of servants, especially of young girls. It's hard to imagine the lives they had; it's easy to think they were all miserable. But they weren't all unhappy. Servants still ended up falling in love and marrying. They had affairs and snuck out to the tavern and got drunk.

Domestic labour was a way for many people to escape agricultural and industrial work. Accommodations and meals were often provided, so falling into a good situation would be significantly better than working in the factories further north. There were opportunities to save. Granted, that was because the work days were so long that servants, especially women, didn't get to leave the house often. Still, some were able to put aside a few pennies and have a small savings for down the road when they married, got sick, or became pregnant.[10]

Nothing says your servants need to be obedient, mild-tempered, simpering middle-aged women. Many servants were teenagers and, well, you can just imagine the snark, sarcasm, and half-hearted jobs that happened whenever they were distracted, bored, tired, hungry, restless, flirting, and/or moody.

# Chapter 8: I'm a Business Man

*"I sold flowers. I didn't sell myself. Now you've made a lady of me I'm not fit to sell anything else."*
-Eliza Dolittle, (George Bernard Shaw, *Pygmalion*)

Working in the inner city opened my eyes to an entire other world of self-employment. Bottle pickers rummaged through garbage bins looking for containers to return for deposits. I'd recycle the containers from our organization, too, and would line up with several of my homeless clients to claim a few dollars in change. Some of them were "solid" with the deposit workers and didn't need to have their cans counted. They'd hand in pre-counted bags; no checking needed.

I don't know what it said about me that I always had to stand in line.

Others picked scrap metal to sell. Since most businesses and construction crews locked down their scrap those days to return for their own profit, a lot of shadier acquisition went on. Some did odd jobs, like washing shop windows in the summer and scraping ice from sidewalks in the winter.

The Georgian and Victorian poor also did similar jobs. There were fewer regulations, too, which gave them ample opportunities to find profit, provided that they were willing to get elbow-deep in dog poo.

This chapter is about the outdoor vendors, cleaners, and criminals that your servants will interact with on a daily basis.

These are the types of people Mr. Darcy sought out while looking for Lydia and Wickham. There was a staggering amount of different jobs worked in the streets, stables, and offices. I've picked some of the more interesting and common individuals that our own Martha and Mark might visit or turn into their careers, but if you're looking for a complete list of jobs, *Henry Mayhew's London Poor and London Labourers (Volume 1)* has a pages-long exhaustive list.

## Shopping is a Lady's Best Friend

The market areas were alive with carts, stands, and baskets filled with merchandise for sale. These people didn't own shops and stores; they relied solely on foot traffic through the markets or other high foot-traffic areas.

Groceries could be purchased from the street-sellers. Fish, poultry, game, cheese, fruit, seeds, and greens were all purchasable from various stalls. Anyone in a hurry and not bothered by stopping at a street market could pick up some take-out. Fried fish, hot eels, penny-priced meat pies, baked potatoes, and muffins.

Mayhew also mentions ham sandwiches, and I feel I should point out that he isn't referring to modern, manufactured ham. I once read a Regency romance where the heroine talked about her breakfast of uniformly round, paper-thin slices of deli ham that she could see through. Be gentle on me and just have them use regular ol' ham roasts. Smoked, boiled, broiled, roasted, fried—I don't care, so long as it's not from the grocery store's deli department.

Hot beverages could also be bought, which would be welcomed on cold days. The standard Starbucks was on display, with tea, coffee, lemonade, milk, and water for sale. Also, some stalls sold ginger beer and hot wine for a different treat. I can picture Martha grabbing some coffee on a cold day when she's on her way home to visit her parents.

Street-sellers sold more than food and drinks. Just about

anything needed at home could be picked up. Entertainment items, such as newspapers, old books, and sheets of music were for sale. Chemicals, brushes, buckets, and brooms were all for sale. Paper, pens, and pencils could all be picked up from a vendor. Repair items like needles and buttons were available, along with dog-collars, cups, sawdust, second-hand goods, and . . . tropical fish?!?

Those who lived day-to-day often spent a portion of the previous day's earnings to pick up an item or two from a wholesaler. An enterprising boy might purchase nuts and bags, to then resell bags of nuts outside of a theatre in the evening. A child might pick up some oranges, flowers, or watercress (basically, whatever was plentiful and inexpensive) and resell them to make a penny or two.

The huge variety in incomes and wares created a hierarchy amongst the costermongers selling their wares. Oranges were the "Irishman's harvest." Most of the oranges and nuts sold in London by the Victorian age were often by poor Irish immigrants, or the children of regular, most respectable costermongers. Mayhew noted that, "I found among the English costermongers a general dislike of the Irish[1]."

There were a number of Jews carrying out street trade. It wasn't uncommon to pick up a coconut on a Sunday from a Jewish street merchant, though sometimes young boys of all backgrounds sold them, too[2].

Saturday nights were hopping busy at the London street markets, as the working-class men and women were out deciding what to pick up for Sunday dinner. Mayhew wrote that, "There are hundreds of stalls, and every stall had its one or two lights . . ."

Not everything for sale was above board. Illicit and smuggled goods were sold openly in the London markets, especially just before the turn of the 18th century.

If you're writing a great lady, chances are she will not be hanging out around the market district. Even the lady's maid of a great mistress probably wouldn't be caught in the market looking for a cheap deal and a meat pie. But Martha, working for a middle-class mistress, might venture down to the markets to look for various items. The servants of the house, such as a kitchen maid or a maid-of-all-work, would need to pick up various supplies that weren't being delivered to the house.

Those servants would be heading to the markets for the best prices, for supplies, and for repairs that couldn't be done at the house. Mark might bring his pocket watch, a gift from his grandfather, to the market for repairs because the clock dealer was closed for the weekend . . . and Mark needs to always know the time. So if you're including a servant's point of view, you'll have plenty of opportunity to send her shopping. Now, the real question is would she be the type to bring back all of the change or would she skim a little off the top?

But while the grocers and the repair shops were more likely to see the servants, the retail stops catered to the ladies. Most of the jobs were apprenticed. Milliners made hats, haberdashery stores had all of the frills and fluffs a lady needed to decorate just about anything, parasol stores, boot and shoes stores, bookstores and publishers, glove stores . . . the list goes on!

While the small towns, like the fictional Highbury, had a multi-purpose store, London was the retail capital. As the Victorian age grew on, department stores opened up, with great opportunities for young, fashionable girls to work in *Lady's Wear*, where an upper crust lady might purchase the same pair of gloves that–*gasp*–a clerk's wife might buy. Only a truly diplomatic salesgirl could navigate those tricky waters to higher commissions!

## Dust, Dirt, and Dung

The roads could become filthy with household garbage piling up, so street sweepers (aka garbage truck drivers) were hired. The rich areas obviously had immaculate roadways, while the poorer areas were filthy. In the 1750s, the individual parishes were responsible for hiring the sweepers, so it's not a surprise that poorer regions like Whitechapel's market area had 1385 houses . . . and four scavengers.

The sweepers would come by daily, except Sunday and holidays, and ring their bell. People could bring out their garbage to throw in the carts. Just about anything could end up in those piles, including animal feces, dead cats and dogs, ashes, straw, and human waste. The mixture sold as fertilizer[3].

At night, the night-soil collectors cleaned out the sewer from the privies and cess-pits, especially in the slum areas of the cities without individualized septic systems and sewer systems.[4]

The Dustmen were often a couple of men with a high-sided cart who collected dust from houses, to deposit at a dustyard. A dustyard was a big operation and a large one could employ 150 people. For example, the dust heap of Gray's Inn Lane went for £20,000. Another one in 1848 combined sewage and dust to create an open-air manure factory, where manure cakes were made and sold to farmers and gardeners for 4-5s a cartload.

Families often worked together on a dust heap. The man carted the rubbish in, the boys carried it to their mothers and put it on a wire sieve called a shifter and they'd sort through it looking for rags, bones, coal, cinders, old shoes, and food scraps. These could all be sold for money. Dustman earned good wages; 10s/week and double that if they worked as night-soil men clearing cesspits.

The stench around the pure gatherers might cause your delicate lady to cover her nose for fear of fainting. Pure was basically dog poop. Tanners purchased it by the bucketful, for about 8-10d (1860s), but it might take a day or two to gather enough. Which meant the gatherers had to carry around a bucket of dog do-do all the time[5].

Can you imagine Mark's face when he has to bribe a pure collector for information? He'd probably pay anything just to get away from the foul-smelling wretch.

The Thames attracted many looking for work. Watermen rowed people out to their boats that were anchored in the river, or who rowed people across the river for a fee. (A waterman on land was someone who stood at cab stands and gave water to the horses.) This was a legitimate job and there was no shame helping people with transport. There were multiple docks and piers, where young children could make themselves useful (before they were big enough to be labourers) by running errands, doing odd jobs, and being generally helpful.

However, there were other people who worked the Thames who were the scavengers of the river. Some called themselves "watermen" but they were known to most as mudlarks: those who scrounged in the Thames's mud.

It used to freeze over, but hasn't since Austen's time due to rising temperatures and construction on the river itself. Sewage used to be pumped into the Thames, so it was a bed of disease. There were several cholera outbreaks in the 19th century related to this.

However, the Thames is also a tidal river. At low tide, it was possible to walk out into the mud (sometimes, up to one's thighs) and scrounge for just about anything of value. Coal, copper nails, and iron pieces were most valuable, but there was also rope, bones, and small metal pieces that could be salvaged and resold[6]. The money was barely enough to survive off, just a couple of pence a day, and was worked by all ages, though popular with very poor children.

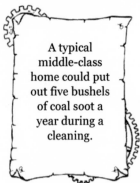

A typical middle-class home could put out five bushels of coal soot a year during a cleaning.

Consider the toll on a body after standing barefoot in muddy water that is not much above freezing temperatures, looking for jagged pieces of scrap. The person would have to be careful that they did not step on anything jagged since they risked sepsis. They'd have to carry a basket or bag to put their findings in and then had to carry it around with them.

Mudlark children were either homeless orphans or children of poor families whose earnings were needed to support the family. The children lived off a pound of bread and a pint of beer for breakfast, and if lucky another pound of bread and a piece of cheese in the afternoon.

Despite the work they did, mudlarks were considered unemployed and thieves, and regularly chased and harassed by security and police.

If the Thames wasn't to your liking, there were always the sewers later on. Rip off the manhole cover and go down to pick through whatever had been flushed away. Can you imagine how badly those people smelled?

The chimneysweep is another horrifying job that was often done by children, including when it was illegal to use children. *Oliver Twist* begins with a disturbing comment about it being humane to light a fire while a child was in the chimney, since it kept them working hard. This wasn't an author's fictional tale; this behaviour did take place. Some of the older kids who worked for a chimney sweep might do just that, or stick the child with pins to get them to work faster. It's where the phrase, "lighting a fire under your behind" comes from. Many were beaten for something as trivial as getting soot on the carpets.

I grew up with a brick chimney in my 100-year-old childhood home. The brick chimney went through the middle of the house. On cold days, I'd hug the chimney to warm up or stick my feet on it for a quick fix.

I was in my early teens when it was pulled down; I have vivid memories of what the chimney looked like. The inside was almost completely smooth and black. Even though our chimney was regularly cleaned, it still had a coating of soot on it. No fire had been lit that day, yet the interior bricks were still warmish.

A child chimney sweep had to use their knees, feet, and elbows to brace themselves as they worked, since there are no hand holds in a chimney. They sometimes had to go up or come down a chimney that was still on fire, in an attempt to put the fire out. If they'd stirred up a lot of soot or smoke—they would if panicking—they risked dying in the chimney.

These kids generally weren't paid, either. All of the money went to their master, leaving them to beg from customers for pennies.

In 1832, Parliament outlawed using climbing boys as young as four or five to crawl into 12 x 14 chimneys (some were as small as 7 inches square)[7]. Children continued to be used, however, until the late 19th century, and many died from various cancers caused by inhaling and touching the carcinogenic coal soot on a daily basis.

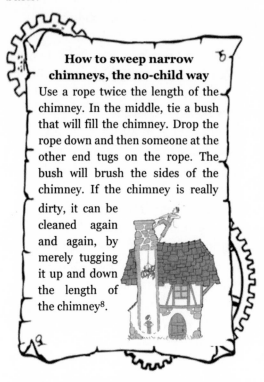

**How to sweep narrow chimneys, the no-child way**
Use a rope twice the length of the chimney. In the middle, tie a bush that will fill the chimney. Drop the rope down and then someone at the other end tugs on the rope. The bush will brush the sides of the chimney. If the chimney is really dirty, it can be cleaned again and again, by merely tugging it up and down the length of the chimney[8].

Does your heroine know that the puny boy scrubbing out her chimney had been purchased for the cost of her pet terrier? Since the soot was carcinogenic and the job very dangerous, many of these children never lived to see the end of their apprentice contracts and freedom. Would Martha's mistress protest that, or would she even notice a problem with it? After all, those children had jobs and weren't starving. Besides, childhood was for the privileged, was it not?

## Randomly Awesome Jobs

Okay, so these jobs aren't related to each other in the slightest. There's no good place to put them; I tried and tried to come up with some artificial classification and I couldn't. Nevertheless, I needed them in this book. They are just too awesome to leave out. I can't read them without thinking of a dozen ways to include them in stories. I hope you can find jobs for these men in your books, too.

Arguably the best named job ever was the knocker-upper. No, not that, you bunch of perverts. Clocks and watches were expensive, and people were exhausted from long work hours. How did they know to get up? The knocker-upper!

This was a man who owned a timepiece, either his own investment or a family heirloom or gift for some extraordinary service. He had a long cane and a lantern, and would wander the streets all night and the early morning, tapping on the windows of his clients. Clients paid a penny a month for his services, and in exchange they were able to get to work on time.

Even small towns that had breweries, a few workshops, and railway construction had enough early-morning workers to employ a knocker-upper[9].

Can you imagine how grumpy Mark would be if a new knocker-upper rapped on his window at 3am instead of his neighbour's!

Like most cities, London had a vermin problem. Ratcatchers were in need, and it was a fun job for a young boy with no education who hated sitting still. The ratcatcher might use arsenic, though in some cases that might risk poisoning animal feed or household pets. A ferret could be used to chase the rats out of the holes in the walls, and a well-trained dog could kill the rats as they tried to escape. More justification for your hero to have a ferret on his airship!

People, I've given your hero permission to own a ferret. Go forth and ferret.

## Reuse, Repurpose, Recycle

Recycling is a strange thing to include in a chapter on jobs. Except that, in the Victorian sense, it was a viable job prospect. It was a good, if unpredictable and unstable, way for the poor to make money. We've already covered some of the jobs that might come across reusable or recyclable items, so this section is to show how those people made money from sewer-soaked rope and rusty nails.

Clothing was a heavily reused and recycled item. The gown worn three times by the Duchess of Importance would be tossed aside because it was unfashionable, itchy, torn, or the lady had gained weight. In many houses, her lady's maid took those dresses, which could be sold to a used clothier, thereby earning both the lady's maid and the clothier money.

Unusable gowns could be turned into underclothing, especially if they were simple and made of wool, but permanently stained. Used clothing sellers were also important, especially for warm, cheap clothing. A woman could repair any holes and then sell. Satins and other expensive clothes rarely came their way and rarely sold well. Cotton and wool sold very well to the price conscious.

Shreds of fabric were sold to the rag-and-bone man, who picked out linen and resold it to paper manufacturers. The bones were ground up for fertilizer (aka bone meal) and sold.

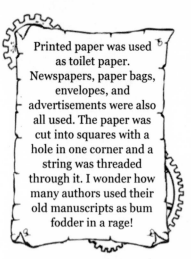

Printed paper was used as toilet paper. Newspapers, paper bags, envelopes, and advertisements were also all used. The paper was cut into squares with a hole in one corner and a string was threaded through it. I wonder how many authors used their old manuscripts as bum fodder in a rage!

Now this is one of the things that a mistress of the house needs to be careful about. Some households let the servants keep their own rag and bone bucket, where they were trusted to only throw out the greasy rags and thrice-boiled bones. The servant would sell their bucket of items, thereby making a few pennies on the side. A grander house or a mean house who didn't treat and pay their servants fairly might not do this. They shouldn't be surprised when the fine table linens disappear more quickly than they should.

For the desperate or the bored, they could strip children. Sometimes children were needed to help a servant bring laundry or ironing to someone's house. If the child got separated from the adults, they could be snatched and stripped bare in seconds. The child would be left naked in the streets, and the aggressor could later sell the

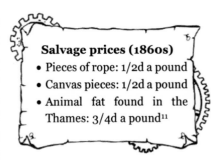

**Salvage prices (1860s)**
- Pieces of rope: 1/2d a pound
- Canvas pieces: 1/2d a pound
- Animal fat found in the Thames: 3/4d a pound[11]

clothing either as second-hand clothes or for rags.

Used tea leaves cleaned the carpets, or could go to the char-woman, who sold them to dealers who added some colours and might recycle them as "tea." Dripping (fat from roasted animals) was sometimes given to the cook or housekeeper. Drippings were purchased for 3 ½ d to 5d (1850s price) and then resold as a butter substitute to the poor. Chimney soot was sold and turned into manure and insect killer.

Metal purchasers could resell their metal directly to manufacturers for (1850s prices per pound[12]):
- copper, 6d;
- pewter, 5d;
- brass, 5d;
- iron 6lbs for 1d, 8lbs for 2d;
- lead, 1 lb.

Public areas were picked clean. Cigar butts were picked up and the tobacco recycled into new cigars. And remember the dog pure guy? That "pure" was sold to tanners to process the kid gloves worn by the upper crust at fancy operas and balls.[10]

Metal (copper, brass, and pewter were especially profitable) could be remelted or rewrought in some form. Manufacturers purchased metal by the pound, making it too much work for the average household to try to pass along. However, it was a perfect business opportunity for someone with a cart. If they had a horse or a donkey, even better, because they could visit the rural areas, too.

## Street-Performers

The streets were alive with performers, artists, and showmen.

121

Puppet shows were popular, especially in the Georgian times. There were also what today we'd consider circus acts, with jugglers, sword-swallowers, clowns, and tight-rope walkers all performing for pennies.

There were also the musically inclined. Professional whistlers, singers, and musicians literally sang for their supper. There were individuals who sang "nigger melodies." Mayhew interviewed a self-described "Ethiopian serenade" who estimated that there were forty or so black men who sang for money in London, beyond a couple of larger groups who performed regularly[13].

One oddity I came across was rifle shooting as a street performance. Can you imagine that in a busy city?

## Working With Disabilities

It was hard enough for able-bodied, healthy individuals to find work. Physical disabilities added even more of a challenge. Mayhew interviewed several disabled street merchants, performers, and general workers to learn more about their lives. As ever, Mayhew's work needs to be read through a filter, but I've picked two stories that show the dedication and drive to keep going.

The **nutmeg-grater seller** sold the wares made by a housemate. He was unable to stand and walked on his knees, so he covered his knees with leather caps. He sold graters and funnels. He paid for his rent daily (1s6d weekly), as well as hired someone to dress and undress him. If it was a rainy day, he went hungry unless someone gave him something to eat. If he felt faint when working, he'd buy a ½d orange. He'd crawl up to two miles in a work day. He suffered from bouts of depression when he was out of work, so tried to always be out, or have someone with him to talk to him and keep him company.

The **profile-cutter** was a cheerful, blind thirty-one-year-old man who cut figures and profiles from paper. He'd lost his sight due to childhood measles. It had come and gone a few times, until it finally left him mostly blind and only able to distinguish different types of light out of one eye. He'd been apprenticed to be a painter, so the loss of his vision put him into the workhouse. There, he endured thirteen eye operations in two years.

Once out of the workhouse, he sold small items, like bootlaces, but made very little at it. He tried making items, but kept cutting himself. Finally, he took up cutting out profiles of animals, birds, and people. He brought in a stunning 30s a week for over a month, before the police ordered him to move along because his work attracted crowds. Eventually, he found a location where the police would allow him to work and, when Mayhew interviewed him, he'd been there for seven years by the Waterloo Bridge. He worked every day, except Sundays, all year round in any weather.

He'd hear the heckling of people crossing the bridge, and could tell by their accents they were middle to upper class folks. The lower classes and the working poor bought his profiles and were the bulk of his customers. He averaged about 8s a week.

## Legal Shmegal

In *What Kings Ate and Wizards Drank*, I talked about illegal ways travelers could earn free meals. The reader comments I got about those sections didn't surprise me. Many people confessed they had not even considered illegal activities. Those things are always put under the "crime and punishment" sections. We aren't used to hearing about them as "jobs."

However, this was a world where rehabilitation wasn't a part of the judicial system. In Tothill Fields Bridewell Prison, children were held for two weeks for stealing 6d or less worth of goods. By today's standards, that's comparable to imprisoning a ten-year-old for two weeks for stealing a couple of chocolate bars.

There were some religious people who believed in predeterminism (that is, the fate of an individual had already been determined by God). There were some people who were just born bad, and they were usually poor. Nothing better could be expected of them. Take that culture, add in meager to no education, unattended youths for long hours of the day, no opportunities for social mobility, and it's no wonder that crime was as popular a choice as it was.

Burglary was a capital crime. English law in the 18th century was based around the notion that the Englishmen's home was his castle. It was considered self-defence to kill a housebreaker, even if they weren't threatening you.

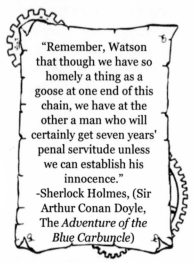

"Remember, Watson that though we have so homely a thing as a goose at one end of this chain, we have at the other a man who will certainly get seven years' penal servitude unless we can establish his innocence."
-Sherlock Holmes, (Sir Arthur Conan Doyle, The *Adventure of the Blue Carbuncle*)

Housebreakers were young, often boys in their late teens. Many started earlier by "theft."

So, if a window, for example, was left unlocked or opened, a thief could use a hook on a stick to lift items out of the house. This was not housebreaking, and while still punishable by law, it did not carry with it a hangman's noose around one's throat[14]. Until fourteen. Then, too bad.

Children under seven could not be found guilty of a crime punishable by death in the 18th century, so they could be trained as thieves. Children between seven and fourteen could only be executed if there was evidence of malice, and after fourteen you were an adult and sucks to be you[15].

Prison wasn't safe, either. In Georgian times, female convicts sentenced to hang could hire a "baby getter" in prison, a man who would try to impregnate her. She could then "plead her belly" to delay execution until her baby was born, or at least until it was certain she wasn't pregnant[16].

In some prisons, however, women didn't need to hire anyone. Clerkenwell Bridewell prison (just outside of London) only fed its female prisoners a penny's worth of bread every day in Georgian times. After all, giving prisoners full stomachs would just encourage more crime. Her choice was risking starving to death or prostituting herself to the male prisoners who tipped the jailer.

At times, she had no say in this choice, and prisoners and guards alike could pass a shilling to her jailer to rape her[17].

# Getting By

Just like there were casual opportunities for domestic service work, there was also services work available. In London, most work was farmed out to households, as opposed to done in factories. That meant that a woman (generally, these jobs were worked by women and girls) could pick up work here and there to do at home when she was unable to do regular work.

Sewing was a popular choice, as all women had some sewing skills no matter their social class. The sewing could take on various forms, including garment finishing. One woman named Isabella Killick was a trouser finisher in London's East End. She sewed pockets, lined trousers, made buttonholes, and sewed on the buttons to trousers. She earned under 1s a day in the 1860s. I can imagine Martha's mother bent close to a candle in front of the fire at night, sewing buttons on trousers and jackets.

Women who had hot water or even laundry facilities might take in laundry from other households. Laundry was a major undertaking, requiring significant time, hot water, and strength. However, everyone had dirty clothes and linens, so there was always need for outside help to get the work done. In the mid to late Victorian age, laundry washers made 2s to 2s 6d for a full day's work.

Clothes also needed ironing and the laundry lady might not have the time or a small girl to help out. The ironing could be sent to someone else to do. An ironer only needed a clean table and a way to heat the iron. It was a long, tedious job, but an ironer could make 3s to 3s 6d on a very busy day[18]. The pay was decent, but it was unpredictable work.

Women took advantage of whatever work was available to them, though most of it paid poorly and wasn't steady.

## Olaudah Equiano (1745-1797)

Olaudah was born in present-day Nigeria. He was kidnapped at the age of eleven. He was eventually purchased by Michael Pascal, a British naval officer, who renamed him Gustavus Vassa (or Vasa).

Equiano came to Britain in 1757 and stayed with Pascal's sisters, who taught him to read. He was sold to various captains before Equiano saved enough to purchase his freedom for £40. Equiano apprenticed as a hairdresser and travelled widely, sometimes as a servant on trans-Atlantic voyages.

Equiano was appointed Commissary of Provisions and Stores for the black poor going to Sierra Leone in 1786. Equiano reported the government agent was committing fraud. The Naval Board sided with Equiano, but the accused was a white man, so the charges were dismissed.

Equiano's participation in the abolition movement was growing. In 1789, Equiano published *The Interesting Narrative of the life of Olaudah Equiano, or Gustavus Vassa, the African*. It was hailed as a "uniquely detailed account of an African's movement out of slavery". It was widely popular and he was quickly recognized as a principal spokesman of Britain's black community[1]. He travelled Britain and Ireland on a book and speaking tour, and addressed anti-slavery meetings.

Equiano did not live to see the end of the African slave trade.

# Chapter 9: Abolition and the Road to Self-Emancipation

*"Africans were in Britain before the British were, marching there with the Roman armies."*
-Peter Fryer, *Staying Power*

I like to share nuggets from my research on social media. Stories from primary source books about prostitution, scrubbing floors, and chimney cleaning. I tell them all. So while I was researching this chapter, I thought nothing of it to share some of the primary source material as well. Wow. I learned a lot about the common misconceptions and preconceptions about this period of England's history.

It's not possible to cover the entire scope of diversity, colonialism, and racism in England in just one chapter. I've decided to narrow it down to the experiences of Africans in Britain and the British-born of African descent.

This section does focus heavily on the African slave trade, since it was the largest. It's important to remember

Historically, "black" people could include Africans, Arabs, North Africans, and South Asians. While most of this chapter does focus on Africans, just keep in the back of your mind that the term "black" (in this case) does encompass a larger group of people than the term covers today.

that Africans were not the only people sold into slavery. Likewise, it's important to recognize the massive impact the African slave trade had on the economy and culture of Europe, Africa, and worldwide—and many of these effects we still see today.

This chapter is about helping writers explore racial diversity in their historical-based fiction. If you're looking for information on Irish indentured servants and white slavery, I recommend *White Cargo* by Don Jordan and Michael Walsh.

# How Many Blacks Were in Britain?

It's impossible to know how many non-white people lived in London; census didn't account for race or colour. Records show that black men and women lived in Britain since at least the 12th century[2]. There were enough for Queen Elizabeth I to order their deportation during a period of famine in the late sixteenth century. The order didn't actually make an impact, and free Africans, West African traders' sons of mixed relations, and imported men and women for domestic servitude continued to stay and work.

There were approximately 10,000 black individuals living in Britain in the 18th century. During the Somerset case in 1772, it was estimated that the black population was 14,000-15,000, with most living in London. A century later, many families had stayed in London, while others had moved to the dock areas of Cardiff and Liverpool[3].

Most blacks were household servants or domestic slaves. Most, but not all. They also worked as labourers, seamen, and craftsmen. George Turner made a living in 1710 by sword-fighting. A "surprising Negro" performed as a fire eater between 1751-52 at Charing Cross. There's a record of at least one black hairdresser working in London in 1788. A black man, originally from Nova Scotia, was ordained as a minister in 1785. Joseph Bank's two servants, Thomas Richmond and George Dalton, accompanied him on Captain Cook's first voyage around the world in 1768. An "East Indian Gentoo" conjurer who did card tricks and thought-reading performed at the Bartholomew Fair in 1790[4].

Likewise, black girls and women were the usual domestic staff, plus independent laundry maids, seamstresses, children's nurses, and prostitutes.

Fashionable ladies had black pages until the mid-1700s. Some blacks held respected posts, such as Francis Barber who worked for Samuel Johnson. Most were not this fortunate. These individuals came to Britain as slaves and indentured servants.

Free individuals also advertised their work. In 1750, a South Asian man who spoke six languages advertised for a position as a footman. Some ads expressed a wish to return to their homeland: "A Female Black Servant would be glad to wait on any Lady or Children going to India; she came from thence . . .[5]"

## Slavery: The Crash Course

The African slave trade to England began in the 1570s. There's no evidence that Africans were being sold in England until 1621, but that doesn't mean it wasn't happening; there just isn't any record. For various reasons, the slave population within England remained small until around the 1650s. Changes in social habits, however, caused the slave population to explode after the 1650s. I'm going to narrow in on the two that most impact writers: trendy items and food.

### Everybody wants a little slave boy

As the 1600s progressed and moved into a new century, it became trendy to have an African slave or two amongst one's household staff. In particular, great ladies wanted to add black slaves to their household staff. These were often young boys serving as pages.

Pages wore ornate outfits and fanned the lady of the house, looked after her dogs, and performed other small tasks. Many great ladies posed for paintings with their pages in the background.

Officers on slave ships also brought young black slaves to Britain with them. In Bristol and Liverpool, your hero could tell a slaver captain by the African child following him around.

There are plenty of paintings of aristocratic women with young, black slaves in the background. It's unfortunate that many of these children are cropped out of digital copies, as it creates the illusion that non-whites were either hidden away or non-existent. A (very) short list of these paintings, sketches, and drawings are:

- William Hogarth's *Harlot's Progress*
- George Morland's *The Fruits of the Early Industry and Economy* (1785-90)
- William Redmore Bigg's *The Charitable Lady* (1787)
- Johann Zoffany's *The Third Duke of Richmond Out Shooting with his Servant*[6]

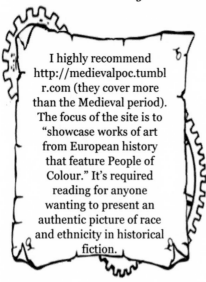

I highly recommend http://medievalpoc.tumblr.com (they cover more than the Medieval period). The focus of the site is to "showcase works of art from European history that feature People of Colour." It's required reading for anyone wanting to present an authentic picture of race and ethnicity in historical fiction.

Oftentimes, the person of colour is painted towards the background or sides of the picture. Modern croppings on popular websites with these paintings, including Wikipedia, sometimes have the person of colour cropped out of the picture. People often think they're looking at the original, when in fact important aspects of race and ethnicity are removed. When looking at paintings of the period for inspiration, make sure you're looking at the full, un-cropped painting or sketch.

## All that's sweet

Three beverages were introduced to wealthy English tables around 1650: tea, chocolate, and coffee. Those three are bitter drinks and there's only one thing that helps the medicine go down—sugar.

Slavery quickly became the fastest, easiest, and most profitable way to have sugar, plus the other foods of the New World. A mercantilist wrote in 1729:

> *If we have no Negroes, we can have no Sugars, Tobaccoes, Rice, Rum, &c . . . consequently, the Publick Revenue, arising from the Importation of Plantation-Produce, must be annihilated: And will this not turn many hundreds of Thousands of British Manufacturers a Begging . . . ?*[7]

Won't someone please think of the poor manufacturers?

## Somerset Case (1771-1772)

I had asked online about something tangentially related to this case, when several people talked about how slavery ended in Britain in the late 1700s. The end of slavery in Britain is tricky because it wasn't just one law and boom, all the slaves were freed. If you are writing during this period, it is very important to double check the slave laws of your location, not to mention how they were being enforced.

Perhaps the biggest reason for this confusion was the Somerset case. So here are the basic details and the aftermath to show why it was a pivotal, but *partial*, victory. And, perhaps more importantly, how the perception and misunderstanding— regardless if it was *intentional* or accidental—was perhaps the watershed moment.

James Somerset was brought to England by Charles Stewart[9], his owner. Somerset escaped while in Britain and was recaptured on November 26, 1771. He was then imprisoned onboard a ship docked in the harbor and was to be transported to Jamaica.

The abolitionists caught wind of this and Granville Sharp took the lead on it. He'd already been working against the changes made to the wordings in the slave laws through a case called the Yorke-Talbot Ruling.

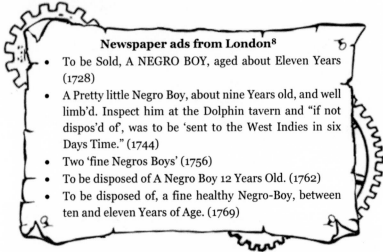

**Newspaper ads from London[8]**

- To be Sold, A NEGRO BOY, aged about Eleven Years (1728)
- A Pretty little Negro Boy, about nine Years old, and well limb'd. Inspect him at the Dolphin tavern and "if not dispos'd of', was to be 'sent to the West Indies in six Days Time." (1744)
- Two 'fine Negros Boys' (1756)
- To be disposed of A Negro Boy 12 Years Old. (1762)
- To be disposed of, a fine healthy Negro-Boy, between ten and eleven Years of Age. (1769)

The Yorke-Talbot Ruling (1729) was made by Attorney General Sir Philip Yorke and Solicitor General Charles Talbot. If Africans were heathens, thereby justifying slavery, then shouldn't the conversion and baptism of said heathen result in their freedom? American colonies began passing laws specifically to deal with that circumstance, but the legal position in Britain was unclear. Yorke and Talbot stated that: "A slave, by coming from the West Indies . . . doth not become free." The ruling goes on to say that baptism does not bestow freedom on the slave. That idea, plus the following, were important for the Somerset ruling:

We are also of opinion, that the master may legally compel him to return to the plantations[10].

A legal team was assembled for Somerset and they argued that slavery was an aspect of local law. Sure, Somerset was a slave in Virginia, but Virginian law had no jurisdiction in England, no more than it did anywhere else. The trial was adjourned for three months. Then, newbie lawyer Francis Hargrave took the floor. He'd never spoken in a courtroom before, and yet laid out an argument based on English contractual law. He argued that English law didn't permit anyone to consensually enslave themselves for life by contract and turned property rights laws against the slavery argument.

Now, this put Lord Chief Justice Mansfield in a bit of a pickle. Hargrave successfully proved his point. He'd shown without

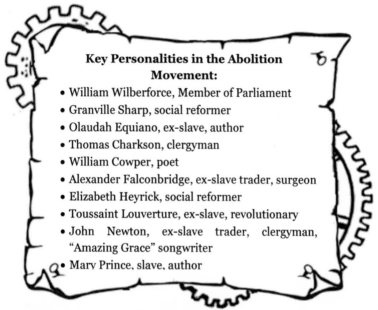

**Key Personalities in the Abolition Movement:**

- William Wilberforce, Member of Parliament
- Granville Sharp, social reformer
- Olaudah Equiano, ex-slave, author
- Thomas Charkson, clergyman
- William Cowper, poet
- Alexander Falconbridge, ex-slave trader, surgeon
- Elizabeth Heyrick, social reformer
- Toussaint Louverture, ex-slave, revolutionary
- John Newton, ex-slave trader, clergyman, "Amazing Grace" songwriter
- Mary Prince, slave, author

doubt that Somerset should be released as a free man. Plus, this Mansfield is the same Mansfield who had a biracial niece living with him; a young woman who'd spent nearly all of her life with her (white) uncle.

But Mansfield didn't want to be the one who issued the order to free the people locked up at the docks in London, Bristol, and Liverpool. The estimated property value of human flesh in England at that time was about £800,000. There was simply too much money at stake.

Lord Chief Justice Mansfield replied to Hargrave and estimated there were no less than 15,000 slaves living in Britain alone (not counting the slaves onboard ships within England waters). He couldn't (read: *wouldn't*) free them all by ruling on property rights.

At the same time, Lord Chief Justice Mansfield wanted a way out for everyone. For Somerset, for Stewart, for himself. He said, "If Mr. Stewart consents to emancipate his slave, there is an end of the matter."

Modern translation? "Dude, take the hint."

He goes on to say, "If, on the contrary, (Stewart) shall insist on demanding a final judgment, we shall not fail to give it faithfully, however irksome and inconvenient[11]."

Then he postponed judgment for another month, hoping someone would slap some sense into Stewart and get him out of the mess of having to rule.

Now, there's some politics going on there behind the scenes. Remember that Yorke-Talbot decision I mentioned? That was the highest legal opinion on slavery at the time, and they were two highly respected lawyers. Mansfield's career successes had been due to the assistance of Yorke and Talbot. Hargrave was a cocky, mouthy youngster who used the sacred property rights laws as a defense of freeing a slave.

*The nerve.*

The easiest thing would have been for Stewart to just free his slave and go away. But Stewart and his backers wanted the courts to rule that blacks were property and kick the abolition movement back a century.

So, in the end, Lord Chief Justice Mansfield couldn't put it off any longer and ruled on June 22, 1772. And ho boy, did he ever check some people's privilege with his (supposed) reply:

> Whatever inconveniences, therefore, may follow from the decision, I cannot say this case is allowed or approved by the law of England; and therefore the black must be discharged[12].

The black community's delegates reportedly bowed to the judge before cheering in celebration. Somerset was released, allowed to live his life as a freeman.

# OK, But What Does This All Mean?

There was confusion even at this time if the Somerset ruling meant that all the slaves should be freed. This ruling didn't end slavery in Britain. It was the turning point, the proverbial writing on the wall.

All that Mansfield had said was that a master could not *by force* compel a slave to leave England. If the slave wanted to go, fine. If the slave was tied up and dragged out of the house, not fine. If the slave said yeah sure, fine. If the slave was beaten so that he couldn't speak, not fine.

The ruling did not end slavery. It made self-emancipation easier, but thousands of people were not freed overnight. Not to mention that people still ignored the law and kidnapped their slaves. Even beyond court cases, there were still witnesses to inhuman treatment.

Thomas Day's poem, *The Dying Negro*, is reportedly based on true events. At the beginning of the poem, he tells the story of an event in 1773 where a black slave ran away, but was subsequently kidnapped by his former master. He was put onboard a ship docked in the Thames bound for America. Not wanting to go back, the man shot himself.

Another example is Hannah Moore (a religious writer) who witnessed, in Bristol in 1790, the seizure of a black woman who didn't want to leave England. She was dragged through the streets and forced onboard a ship[14].

However, these smaller incidents pale in comparison to the very public, very horrific *Zong* massacre. The *Zong* was an English slave ship bound for Jamaica. It left port on September 6, 1781 with 17 crew members and 470 slaves. By late November, 7 crew and 60 slaves had died, and many more slaves were sick.

If slaves onboard died a natural death, such as disease or illness, the ship's crew would have to bear the financial loss themselves. However, if the slaves were thrown overboard for "safety" reasons, insurance would cover it. So, the captain, Luke Colling-wood, concocted a plan to toss the slaves overboard.

Though the mate, James Kelsal, initially opposed the plan, he went along with Collingwood. Slaves were tossed overboard in batches over the next three days. The owners then claimed the full value of the murdered slaves on the grounds of scarcity of water to save the crew.

However, Kelsal stated that the Africans were tossed overboard after a heavy rain and that the ship arrived in Jamaica with spare water. The courts ordered the insurance company to pay £30 per slave, but the insurance refused.

Olaudah Equiano got wind of this and was able to get word to Granville Sharp, who took up a campaign against the owners and pressed for the crew to be investigated for murder.

We don't know if the owners ever got their money or not, but we do know that John Lee, the solicitor-general, personally defended the slave owners. He said:

> This is a case of chattels or goods. It is really so; it is this case of throwing over goods; for to this purpose, and the purpose of the insurance, they are good and property: whether right or wrong, we have nothing to do with[15].

Nothing came of Sharp's campaign to prosecute the crew for murder. However, one small step towards emancipation happened because of this incident. While the law moves slow and it took until 1788, the Dolben's Act was passed to help regulate the slave trade. Then, another law in 1796, where the courts ruled that slaves could no longer be treated as merely merchandise[16].

So, then the Somerset case didn't actually do anything? It's tempting to think this, but it's not true. The Somerset case was a massive turning point in British law. Many scholars believe that the "ruling led to the abolition of the slave trade (1807) and the eventual emancipation of all slaves in the British colonies (1834)"[17]. It was also used in Scottish courts, even though the legal system was different.

## Dido Elizabeth Belle
## (1761 (?) – 1804)

Dido Elizabeth Belle was born in either 1761 or 1763 and reputedly the daughter of Sir John Lindsay, a captain in the Royal Navy, and an enslaved woman rescued from a captive Spanish ship.

Dido was brought up at Kenwood House, the home of her childless great uncle and aunt, Lord and Lady Mansfield. There, she grew up with her cousin, Lady Elizabeth Murray[13]. Dido was technically a slave, as her mother had been one. She was officially granted her freedom in 1793 when her great uncle died.

However, she was not treated as a slave nor servant at the Mansfield home. She had money and chores, but never chores outside of her station as a member of the family. She enjoyed a close relationship with her cousin, Elizabeth.

After the deaths of her father and her great uncle, both men left her money and she was a wealthy woman. Little is known about her life after this point, though it's thought she married a lawyer.

In fact, the decision ended up impacting the American constitution, which added the fugitive slave clause; without it, common law would require escaped slaves be freed[19].

It has never been clear what Mansfield meant or intended as his scope for the ruling. Further, later he made comments that come across as him trying to limit the importance of his very important ruling. Yet, Mansfield after this ruling, along with English judges, constantly upheld the rights of former slaves and not their masters. Because, even then, contemporaries recognized that Somerset basically ended slavery in England . . . even if it actually didn't.

## Okay, So How Did They Free Themselves Before They Were Freed?

Martha's grandfather had self-emancipated himself. While he is a fictional character I created to help with the facts and figures I present, I didn't make up the notion of freeing oneself. There is a common misconception that it was the abolition movement, led by upper middle class and wealthy individuals, which freed all of the slaves. This isn't an accurate picture.

Many slaves arrived in England and, as the *Gentlemen's Magazine* back in 1764 complained, stopped thinking of themselves as slaves, "nor will they put up with an inequality of treatment." They wanted freedom to live their lives, and make choices about what they did with it, just like any other person.

There were ways some slaves could free themselves, just as Martha's grandfather had done. Dr. Douglas Lorimer outlines three ways that slaves self-emancipated themselves[20]. First, some slaves fell into positions that resembled serfdom more than slavery. They were bound to households, but more under serf rules than slave rules, and able to eventually come up from under their situation.

Others used the question of wages to free themselves. If granted wages through a various number of reasons and situations, they were able to achieve some form of independence. In the short term, they could participate in the well-established black communities in London. But also, by demanding wages and being granted them, they were claiming an income, no matter how small. That income, even if it was only ¼d a year, was still an income and gave them the right of residence in an area. Which meant they could get Poor Law relief by the letter of the law if they became free by any means.

Some slaves fought back. They resisted, they fled, and they used the laws in their favor. After Mansfield's ruling, runaway slaves had a measure of protection in the eyes of the law. And we know that slaves ran away because of ads in the newspapers. Plantation owners brought over their long-serving slaves . . . who ran at the first opportunity.

One of the most important ways to challenge the narrative and focus from the white and wealthy abolitionists is to remember that people like Martha's grandfather lived. They were supported by the abolitionists; their personal acts shouldn't be overshadowed.

So if you are writing a scene where your heroine is deciding

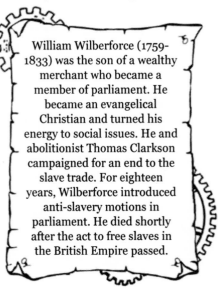

William Wilberforce (1759-1833) was the son of a wealthy merchant who became a member of parliament. He became an evangelical Christian and turned his energy to social issues. He and abolitionist Thomas Clarkson campaigned for an end to the slave trade. For eighteen years, Wilberforce introduced anti-slavery motions in parliament. He died shortly after the act to free slaves in the British Empire passed.

how to help a runaway kid, remember the words of Granville Sharp. In 1785, his brother asked him how best to protect a runaway boy. Sharp recommended not to buy the boy's freedom, but to protect the boy from being kidnapped and re-enslaved. In Sharp's eyes, running away was an act of freeing oneself under the letter of the law.

## Ignatius Sancho (1729 – 1780)

Ignatius Sancho was born on a slave ship on the mid-Atlantic in 1729 and was soon orphaned. When Sancho was three, he was brought to England and given to three unwed sisters, who refused to educate the boy, though he did learn on the sly. Sancho ran away at twenty and sought refuge with the Duke of Montagu, their neighbour. The Duke took him in until his death, when his widow employed Sancho as a butler.

Sancho wrote poetry, plays, songs, minuets, and composed musical arrangements. He also had a wild streak and once lost his clothes gambling! The famous Thomas Gainsborough even painted his portrait.

Eventually Sancho left the Montagus, married, and went on to have six children. The Duchess left him a small legacy and annuity, which he used to open a grocery. Sancho died in 1780 and his writings were published to show that "an untutored African may possess abilities equal to a European.[21]"

# Writing Authentically

Throughout this chapter, I hope that you've seen that black people did in fact exist in England and they had a vibrant history.

They weren't only slaves, but also servants, businessmen, and even one was an aristocrat. It is tempting and easy to write an all-white world when writing history; it's all many of us have been taught. Many of the famous paintings that I've seen in textbooks were all cropped, literally cutting away history until it was whitewashed.

I think we can do better than that in our own books. But where to start? How do we write authentically about people who are cut out of the picture? Well, let's look at what people from the era said and did.

First, let's talk about those young boys serving as pages. There are numerous paintings of great ladies posing with their black pages. The pages did various tasks, like attending his mistress' person and her tea-table. Her train might need carrying as she moved around the house. The page was there to produce her smelling salts and fan, if necessary. He'd feed the parrots and comb her lapdogs.

If you're writing a steampunk set in a world of slavery, consider how that will affect your crew. Will your captain be allowed to disembark from his own ship without being kidnapped? Likewise, what if your hero's steam or air ship docks in a country where slavery isn't legal? Will the ship's slaves be chained up or will he risk the slaves running away?

For a child, this was a "better" life than being chained to a copper pot or being beaten on a plantation. But, in the end, it was servitude. If they weren't being paid, they were owned by another, with no chance to make choices for their own lives. They were slaves.

One of the most iconic moments in English literature is when Elizabeth Bennet visits Pemberley. She walks through a private gallery, depicting the various family members through the generations. If your heroine encounters such a scene, she will see plenty of great ladies and their young slaves. Will your heroine side with the abolitionists? Will her rival anger her by laughing off her concerns about his aunt still keeping a black slave to comb her terrier? Will your hero snap at the woman his mother wants him to marry, accusing her of false kindness; after all, if she really cared about her slave boy, she'd free him while he still had his whole life ahead of him.

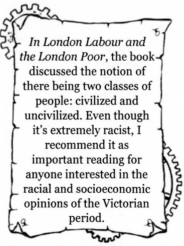

In *London Labour and the London Poor*, the book discussed the notion of there being two classes of people: civilized and uncivilized. Even though it's extremely racist, I recommend it as important reading for anyone interested in the racial and socioeconomic opinions of the Victorian period.

Not all blacks in England were slaves, nor were they all mistreated. Samuel Johnson's black servant, Francis Barber (no longer a slave), had a group of his African countrymen sitting around a fire in the house. It shocked Johnson's visitor, but Johnson had once famously toasted, "here's to the next insurrection of the negroes in the West-Indies." Barber had an employer who treated him like a human being and this meeting seemed to be a regular, sanctioned event within the house[23].

One of the street performers interviewed by Henry Mayhew listed the jobs he'd seen worked by black people:

> The 'niggers' that I know have been errand-boys, street-niggers, turf-cutters, coalheavers, chandlers, paviours, mud-larks, tailors, shoemakers, tinmen, bricklayers' labourers, and people who had no line in particular but their wits . . . Some niggers are Irish. There's Scotch niggers, too. I don't know a Welsh one, but one of the street nigger-singers is a real black – an African[24].

Your soldier hero might surprise his family by telling stories about black drummers. All of the drummers for the 7 Royal

Fusiliers were black men. The Buckinghamdshire Militia had a black tambourinist and a black cymbalist in their band in 1790. A black man was discharged in 1823 from the 1thst Foot Guards for not looking "black" enough.[25]

While there were clearly opportunities, the colour of one's skin did impact one's future. One of Equiano's employers suggested he go to Africa as a missionary, but the bishop of London refused to ordain him. Another man was unable to find work as a Schoolmaster or teacher in any form in 1815 because of his "so dark a complexion."[26] This would make it difficult for Martha's brothers to get middle-class positions because their skin colour would be a hindrance.

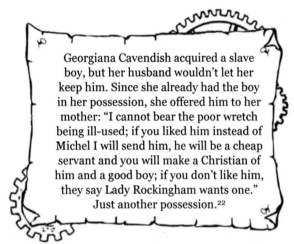

Georgiana Cavendish acquired a slave boy, but her husband wouldn't let her keep him. Since she already had the boy in her possession, she offered him to her mother: "I cannot bear the poor wretch being ill-used; if you liked him instead of Michel I will send him, he will be a cheap servant and you will make a Christian of him and a good boy; if you don't like him, they say Lady Rockingham wants one." Just another possession.[22]

How would your heroine react to her family taking her to see albinos or the "spotted negro boy?" What about Saartjie Baartman? Saartjie was put on display for her large buttocks and Regency gawkers paid 2s a ticket in 1810 to view her. Would your hero agree with *The Times* when they complained she was being treated like a wild animal? Will your heroine be writing anonymous letters to the *Morning Post*, complaining Baartman was being displayed like "a prize ox?"

How do you think Martha would react if her mistress's visiting niece required Martha to accompany her to go view Baartman on display? Would she go silently, or would she quit her position?

Would she beg her mistress not to send her, or would she be too afraid to not find as good of a job to speak up?

Of course, not every heroine is a fine lady dressed in muslin. What would your white mistress think of her lady's maid sneaking off to an African dance in London? Would she be upset by it, or would she give her the 12p (1787) admission cost? How about the (partial) victory party after the Somerset case? Tickets were 5s each, and 200 men and their ladies attended.

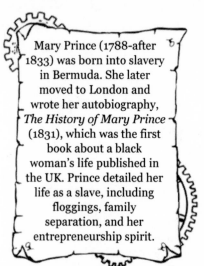

Mary Prince (1788-after 1833) was born into slavery in Bermuda. She later moved to London and wrote her autobiography, *The History of Mary Prince* (1831), which was the first book about a black woman's life published in the UK. Prince detailed her life as a slave, including floggings, family separation, and her entrepreneurship spirit.

What about the 4am party in February 1764? *The London Chronicle* wrote that, "On Wednesday night last no less than fifty seven of them (Blacks servants), men and women, supped, drank and entertained themselves with dancing and music . . . in a public house in Fleet Street till four in the morning. No whites were allowed to be present."[27]

A lady attending an opera might see "men of colour in the rank of gentlemen" swapping stories. Or, a black lady, "cover'd in finery" at the opera. A white American visitor to London wrote about his disapproval of seeing a fashionable black man escorting a white woman on his arm down the road . . . and that the couple was left alone by the crowd to carry on in this fashion[28].

There were more black men than women, so there was a significant amount of intermarriage within one's own social sphere. There were people who noted that poor women seemed fine with unions with black men. Many blacks were poor and, chances are, their partners were equally poor. It seems, for example, that some of the white women who journeyed to Sierra Leone in 1787 were prostitutes[29].

As always, that brings out the racists. Edward Long, a white

Jamaican writer in 1772, wrote that:

> The lower class of women in England, are remarkably fond of the blacks, for reasons too brutal to mention . . . By these ladies they generally have a numerous brood. Thus in the course of a few generations more, the English blood will be so contaminated by the mixture and from the chances, the ups and downs of life, this alloy may spread too extensively, as even to reach the middle, and then the higher orders of the people, till the whole nation resembles the Portuguese . . . in complexion of skin and baseness of mind[30].

Poor Edward.

Even after slavery was illegal, people still broke the law. In 1822, Mrs. Allen of Antigua came to England with her slave, Grace Jones, and returned to Antigua a year later. Jones was seized by a customs officer, arguing that Jones was a free British citizen and had been imported illegally[31].

Some upper class folks tolerated the poor intermarrying; poor was poor, no matter the race. Others saw intermarriage as the end of whiteness, the end of the world, etc. etc. and etc. Still more used "science" to show that the African was a stupid, brutish savage that needed Christianity[32].

John Ocansey, a black travelling in 1881, said he was generally well-treated but that he understood there was a certain attitude towards Africans that was uncomfortable, sometimes insulting. He had no desire to be in a position where he had to defend his people.[33]

Even though slavery was outlawed in Britain by the time Mark is hunting for spies and saboteurs, he'd have to face his own prejudices. Will he automatically suspect anyone with a darker skin than his own, or will he stick with just the facts? And what about his superiors that he's reporting to? Will they just assume the "negro" did it, or will they also demand proof?

I'm going to end with Sancho's words. He taught himself to read and write as a child, since the ladies who owned him believed "to enlarge the mind of their slave would go near to emancipate his person." And while his letters are rarely bitter or downtrodden, he does say, "To the English, from Othello to Sancho the big – we are either foolish – or mulish – all – all without a single exception[34]."

## Moll King's Coffee House

Not much can be confirmed about Moll King's (1696?-1747) early years. She was most likely imprisoned a few times, and might have even been transported for a few years. She was probably a pickpocket and a thief, as well as a prostitute in her younger days. Various pamphlets with exaggerated claims were published about her, and it's widely rumoured that Daniel Defoe based *Moll Flanders* partially on her.

Moll King and her husband, Tom, opened the all-night Tom King's Coffee House. It quickly became a meeting place for prostitutes and their clients. The coffee house didn't have any beds for use, so it wasn't a brothel. Moral campaigners were constantly infiltrating Tom and Moll's coffee house, but they never broke the letter of the law.

Tom passed away in 1739 from the effects of alcoholism, leaving Moll with an estate and a lot of money. She decided to keep on running what was now called Moll King's Coffee House. She spent three months in prison due to the coffee house being the epicentre of a riot, but her nephew bribed the guards so much that she was quite comfortable in jail. She retired to her row of houses in 1745 until her death, dying a wealthy and propertied woman.

# Chapter 10: Whores, Wenches, and Women

*"I had command enough of head to break properly to his the course of life that the consequences of my separation from him had driven me into . . . he was the less shocked at; as, on reflecting how he had left me circumstances, he could not be entirely unprepared for it."*
-Fanny Hill to Charles, her long-lost love, telling him that his abandonment had caused her to turn to prostitution to support herself (John Cleland, *Fanny Hill*)

Sex.

Now that I have your attention. When I first announced *Hustlers, Harlots, and Heroes*, folks really narrowed in on the "harlots" in the title. I think it's because the world of Jane Austen is sanitized in her novels, and even more so in the movie and television adaptations. Even something as simple as, "was Mr. Darcy a virgin" has caused huge internet arguments.

I should know; I started a few of them.

This chapter will focus on prostitution, be it the high-priced courtesans, the addicted street walkers, to the gay "molly houses". You won't find the standard dos and don'ts of the era here. Nearly every etiquette book written about the Regency is filled with absolute social rules that, in reality, were only followed by a select social stratum, and only by some of those people. Instead, let's explore the realities of sex work in the age of contradiction.

## Sin City

London was famous for its sheer number of prostitutes. Eighteenth century London had more openly working prostitutes than anywhere in Europe. It was estimated that one Londoner in five was involved in the sex industry in some fashion. A former rake in 1758 calculated there were as many as 62,500 prostitutes, though one assumes he didn't visit each of them to confirm the number.[1]

Prostitution was *everywhere*.

There were all social levels of prostitutes, from high-priced courtesans to alcoholic, destitute women who'd exchange sex for gin. Some women sat at home with their door or window open, as a sign that they were available. (Learning this fact has made my own mother's obsession with me never standing near a window make so much more sense.) Some even made sexual gestures or exposed themselves.

Dr. Hallie Rubenhold perhaps best described the Regency period with this:

> In the twenty-first century it is often fashionable to bemoan the world we have lost, one devoid of *Big Brother* and the publicized sex stunts of celebrities. But the pages of the *Harris's List* demonstrate that we cannot search for our innocence in the era of Jane Austen, either[2].

Jane Austen herself joked about prostitution on a trip to London: "I should inevitably fall a Sacrifice to the arts of some fat Woman who would make me drunk with small beer[3]." It was easy for Austen to joke about this, since such a fate would never fall to her. For one in five women, it wasn't a joke. It was what they did, either by choice, necessity, or force.

First, let's look at choice. A young woman with a bit of beauty and quick wit could command £2 a night for one man to stay with her in the 1790s. Let's say she only worked three nights a week. That's £6 a week. She'd need decent lodgings, food, fuel, alcohol (for company), and clothing, but wants to work as an independent and not under a bawd. Let's say that sets her back £2 a week,

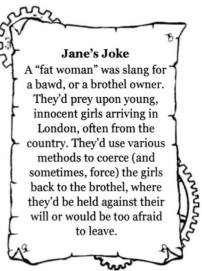

**Jane's Joke**
A "fat woman" was slang for a bawd, or a brothel owner. They'd prey upon young, innocent girls arriving in London, often from the country. They'd use various methods to coerce (and sometimes, force) the girls back to the brothel, where they'd be held against their will or would be too afraid to leave.

which was an outrageous sum, but she wanted decent lodgings and food. That still leaves her £4 a week. At her age, that's not much less than what she'd earn in a year scrubbing floors as a maid-of-all-work and ruining her health.

Prostitution did have a glamorous appeal to some young girls; no different than pop stars and actresses do today. Courtesans travelled in fancy carriages, wore *silk* dresses, and supported themselves with their own work. They were already considered fallen and outside of the rules, so they lived however they wanted. That could have a lot of appeal to a restless sixteen-year-old faced with drudgery and poverty.

As I go into this chapter, a lot of it is going to be very sad. Girls who were victims of rape were tossed out, had nowhere to go, and turned to prostitution to eat. And soon turned to the gin bottle to cope. That was a common enough story, but it wasn't the only one.

A young, pretty girl risked sexual molestation at every turn as a maid. She risked being fondled by members of the household, being seduced by male visitors, and raped by other employees in the house. Her virtue was already at peril. An enterprising girl might decide it was better to choose who took her virtue, as opposed to worrying about it being a dark shadow. And, if she could make some money out of the deal, all the better.

Martha's mother would be all too aware of the dangers of sending her girls out to work. Her girls would need to work; money doesn't grow on trees. However, she would try her best to keep her girls in good homes, or near to home as much as possible. Martha would be very fortunate, because her parents would be able to take her back home for a month or two if she had to leave her employment because she was being harassed. Many girls didn't have that luxury.

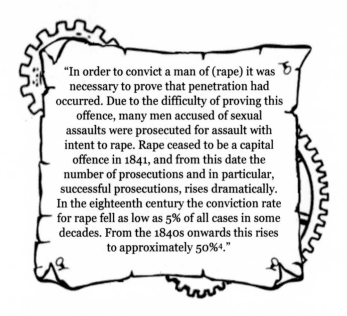

"In order to convict a man of (rape) it was necessary to prove that penetration had occurred. Due to the difficulty of proving this offence, many men accused of sexual assaults were prosecuted for assault with intent to rape. Rape ceased to be a capital offence in 1841, and from this date the number of prosecutions and in particular, successful prosecutions, rises dramatically. In the eighteenth century the conviction rate for rape fell as low as 5% of all cases in some decades. From the 1840s onwards this rises to approximately 50%[4]."

Some girls and women entered prostitution out of necessity. Some married women engaged in casual prostitution when they needed money. Perhaps their husbands were injured or drunk, sick or lazy. It didn't matter. If she couldn't get sewing or laundry work, she might resort to a few nights of sex work. Street prostitutes didn't make the kind of money that the housed, young things charged, but a shilling was a shilling.

It was dangerous work, though. A woman risked rape, robbery, and assault when she worked the streets at night. Many spent a goodly portion of their earnings on cheap gin to help them cope through the indignity they felt. That was a dangerous path, since addiction could easily take over and put the woman into a vicious cycle of self-abuse.

Many girls, especially young girls, entered prostitution because they had no other viable option due to rape, seductions, or consensual sexual activity.

There was a medical belief that a female's sexuality awakened on her wedding night with her husband. Then, her sexual appetite would overtake that of her husband's, unless he controlled her. If a girl had sex before marriage, then it stood to reason that she would be unable to control herself and would be sexually available to anyone.

Reputation could be preserved in the case of rape or sex, provided no one knew and it could be hushed up. However, if a girl became pregnant and was found out before an abortion was obtained, many of those girls turned to the sex trade for survival.

Finally, many young women, especially in Georgian times, didn't just end up on the streets. Most did not go from scrubbing floors at a middle-class house to standing in back alleys selling themselves. They often fell victim to a bawd. Until 1835, the most common way a girl entered the trade was a bawd or her bullies.

> "It is a popular misconception . . . that the respectable Victorian woman was prudish and uninterested in sex . . . (Period literature) openly acknowledged that young married women took great pleasure in having sex with their husbands."
> –Ruth Goodman

The bawd sought out isolated, vulnerable, pretty girls (some as young as twelve) and charmed their way into the girl's confidence. Or, intimidated their way in there. Once a girl was brought back to the brothel and locked in, she only had to be told that her parents would never have her back. Lies upon lies were told, girls were given a meal and some clothes, and then told they had to pay for it or the constables would be called.

Virgins fetched higher prices, willing or not. A girl could pass as a virgin for several months, fetching premium rates. One brothel that catered to the higher end of society charged fifty guineas for a virgin, whereas the everyday ladies charged £5 a night.[5]

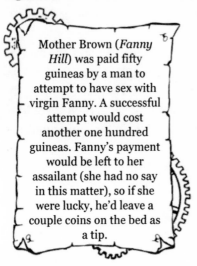

Mother Brown (*Fanny Hill*) was paid fifty guineas by a man to attempt to have sex with virgin Fanny. A successful attempt would cost another one hundred guineas. Fanny's payment would be left to her assailant (she had no say in this matter), so if she were lucky, he'd leave a couple coins on the bed as a tip.

Getting fresh blood was a very solid business model, and a greedy, unscrupulous bawd would have no problem abducting girls. It was one of the reasons they were so reviled. And though abduction wasn't the most common path to sex work (poverty was), it has always received the most airtime.

In 1752, a report was published about Mary Parkington, sixteen years old. Her father was dead, and her mother was remarried. She had been seduced by a naval officer, who left her a couple days later.

Mary was afraid to go home and had no money. A bawd took her in. Mary was given clothes. The bawd wrote her a note (like an IOU or an invoice) for £5. Mary was then prostituted to several men. Excepting a few shillings left as tips, all of the money went to the bawd. Mary was kept against her will in the house and forced into these sex acts because of the £5 IOU. She was told (incorrectly) that, if she escaped, the police would arrest her and send her to Newgate Prison. Chances were the Gaol Fever would kill her there.

Sadly, the pamphlet doesn't say what ever happened to young Miss Mary.

Mayhew interviews a Victorian girl who became a child prostitute. She was a "good-looking girl of sixteen" who had become a maid-of-all-work at ten years of age. She was sent to a home where the mistress of the house beat her. Three weeks into her employment there, the girl's mother died, making her an orphan. She stayed on at the house for another six months before the beatings became too much. She ran away with three shillings to her name.

She was in and out of jail for various reasons, including a month in jail for stealing a piece of beef. She "took up with" a fifteen-year-old boy until he was sent to prison. She lived on the streets off and on for three years, taking up shared lodgings with gangs of young people who stole and prostituted themselves. She said many of the girls were

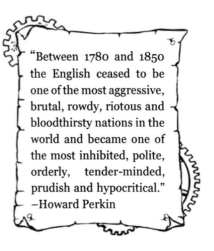

"Between 1780 and 1850 the English ceased to be one of the most aggressive, brutal, rowdy, riotous and bloodthirsty nations in the world and became one of the most inhibited, polite, orderly, tender-minded, prudish and hypocritical."
–Howard Perkin

beaten by their boyfriends if they didn't earn enough money from prostituting themselves[6].

When writing your hero visiting brothels and seeking out prostitutes, consider the workers' feelings and situations. A hero like Mark might love the ladies, but he'd be self-aware enough to understand that many of these girls ended up in the brothels through no fault or choice of their own. Likewise, when someone like Martha walks down an alley and sees rag-clad, shriveled women selling their bodies for a quick drink, she'd probably press a spare coin into the girl's hand to save her a brute's hands for a few hours at least.

Prostitution was glamorous for some of the lucky ones. For the majority, sex work was a necessity just to survive.

## The Ladies of Covent Garden

The *Harris's List of Covent Garden Ladies* was published from 1757 to 1795 and was an annual listing of some of the prostitutes in the Covent Garden area. It sold thousands of copies annually. It listed 120-200 prostitutes, their appearance, their addresses, their inclinations, and their prices.

Was it a real listing of real ladies of the night, or was it merely meant for male fantasy during their alone time? Scholars debate this. Hallie Rubenhold, an expert in the Harris Lists, points out that they were written for men, and not women, so even if the stories were real, they would have been significantly changed for the male audience.

However, the stories told in the list—real, imaginary, or half-truths—paint an interesting picture of how prostitution looked during this flamboyant period of history.

There were the sad stories, such as Miss Bro-n (many of the names were partially obscured). "The situation of this lady is truly pitiable, for as we understand, her heart was betrayed by a young gentleman in the country, who soon forsook her[7]."

Or what about Miss Lef-r. She had been a servant in a gentleman's family. However, "a certain gentleman of the law" found her to be a very fine girl. He followed her and chatted her up, and eventually persuaded her to make tea for him in his room. There, he raped her and deserted her. "The consequences of which was, having lost her place, and being destitute of a character, she was obligated to have recourse to her beauty for a subsistence[8]."

Child prostitute Kitty Buckley of Poland Street had been "at the service of every man that has a mind to her, from her thirteenth year[9]."

Mrs. Ha-on of Queen Ann Street was debauched by a Scotch gentleman of the army. However, he'd found an opportunity to marry, so left her with a *small present*.

Some of the stories are quite cheeky. Mrs. P-age, for example, was twenty and had been in the business since she was fifteen. She was not of a "mercenary disposition" though she did expect to be paid £1.1s. Though if her client was cheap, she'd put up with half her usual rate than go without any trade[10].

Miss J-nson near the Dog and Duck was low-spirited and required a lot of liquor to brighten her spirits. She probably would end up in the lowest class of prostitutes, but she was still young, so there was hope. Perhaps an amateur would take a fancy to her pretty face and rescue her from prostitution[11].

And the stories go on. There are several tales throughout the various lists about "exotic" women, for those men tired of white women. There were the specialists, of course, who serviced women as well as men, who "used the birch" on anyone needing punishment, and a few who were available for elderly gentlemen's needs. The list was quick to point out when the carpet matched the drapes (they say that, only slightly more vulgar), and anyone who was loud, swore more than necessary, and who laughed too much.

I've read a couple of the different Harris's Lists, as well as

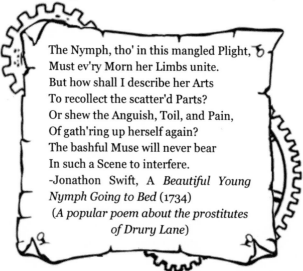

The Nymph, tho' in this mangled Plight,
Must ev'ry Morn her Limbs unite.
But how shall I describe her Arts
To recollect the scatter'd Parts?
Or shew the Anguish, Toil, and Pain,
Of gath'ring up herself again?
The bashful Muse will never bear
In such a Scene to interfere.
-Jonathon Swift, A *Beautiful Young Nymph Going to Bed* (1734)
(*A popular poem about the prostitutes of Drury Lane*)

Rubenhold's excellent edition, and I find myself wondering how would some of our romantic heroes react to such a book. Would our French airship captains scramble to find the nearest docking station to Drury Lane or Covent Garden, in hopes of finding these women? Would our army scoundrels tell jokes about the time they did Covent Garden?

And what about our heroines? Would they be disgusted or would they faint with horror? Or, would they shrug and ask the gentlemen present, "Well, good sir, what do you expect those poor wretches to do once abandoned by their lovers?"

## The Contagious Diseases Acts

I spent way too much of my undergrad studying the Contagious Diseases Acts. I can't say exactly why they appealed to me, but they always have.

The CD Acts, as they were known, were passed in 1864, 1866, and 1869. Venereal disease was rife throughout the British army. The first Act was passed to give police officers the power to arrest prostitutes in various towns and force them to be checked for disease. If infected, she would be put into a lock hospital until cured.

The purpose being to control the spread of disease amongst the troops. However, the prostitutes' clients, either military or otherwise, weren't subjected to any forced examinations. They also weren't subject to months locked up in hospitals.

Butler also belonged to a group which forced parliament to raise the age of consent from 13 to 16, in an attempt to curb child prostitution.

Josephine Butler (1828-1906) led the repeal against the Acts, even as proposals were being tabled to extend the acts even further, giving police even more control over the bodies of women. Butler was an outspoken social justice advocate for women, especially prostitutes. She was a devout Christian who was able to reconcile that, while she considered sex work a sin, those women still deserved fair treatment. She pointed out the double standards of sexual morality in the Victorian era, showing how it punished poor women and rewarded men of all ranks.

Plus, being accused of having a VD often put these women out of work, even if they were clean. They'd have to leave their area or turn to more dangerous and less financially lucrative options.

Butler spoke at open meetings about what she called "surgical rape" and described the process of what happened to these accused women. Very unladylike for a woman from upper middle-class roots.

Butler and her co-campaigners argued that the laws removed "the legal safeguards hitherto enjoyed by women in common with men." They pointed out these women were being forced to "put their reputation, their freedom, and their persons" into the total power of the police. And they called attention to the glaring double standard:

> Because it is unjust to punish the sex who are the victims of a vice, and leave unpunished the sex who are the main cause, both of the vice and its dreaded consequences; and we consider that liability to arrest, forced medical treatment, and (where there is resisted) imprisonment with hard labour, to which these Acts subject women, are punishments of the most degrading kind[12].

Butler faced the public, threats, health problems, and her own husband's career set-backs because of her unladylike behavior. Nevertheless, she toured the country and spoke publicly about sexuality, venereal disease, and prostitution, shocking many. In 1883 the Acts were suspended, with them officially being re-pealed in 1886.

## Homosexuality, Prostitution, and the Law

Consensual sex between men was a capital crime until 1861, punishable by hanging. The law didn't focus on sexual orientation or using a label to define the person who engaged in sodomy. A man committed the act. Nothing more. It wasn't until the late 19th century that the concept of punishing the *homosexual* came about.[14]

Gay clubs and brothels existed underground through the Georgian and Victorian eras. It was thought in Georgian times that reporting on sodomy arrests and convictions would just make the crime more likely to happen again. Giving space to talk about the act meant that it would just give more people the idea to do it[15]. There was a shift after 1820, when newspapers ran hundreds of articles about sodomy, sex between men, and homosexuality (the labels changed, but the stories were the same).

There are a lot of court cases and the notes and goings on were all recorded for anyone to read. Some of them had families saying horrible things in court about their family member being charged with sodomy or homosexuality; yet, what was said in court wasn't always reflective at home.

Families reacted differently to finding out a family member was gay, just like today. In my own lifetime, I've witnessed the entire gambit, from downright denial, "don't ask don't tell" mentality, abuse and rejection from the family, open acceptance, and helpful grandmothers trying to find their gay grandson a good-looking husband.

That isn't a modern invention. Families have always behaved like that. Some kept it secret, some helped facilitate relationships, and some families banished and punished their family members. But then you read stories of people like John Joyce. He was arrested for sodomy and his name and the details of his arrest were published in *The Times*. He was convicted and exiled for a decade.

His sister, Johanna Carrington, never turned her back on him. She took on a letter-writing campaign to help his return to England. When he was finally released, she financially helped him. Johanna even offered to take him in upon his release, if he needed it, even though it would have caused her public grief.

> In *Mansfield Park*, Mary Crawford says "of rears and vices, I saw enough." Miss Crawford is talking about admirals, but also it's a play on words. Jane Austen's brother, Frank, served aboard a Royal Navy ship that had an unfortunate outbreak of homosexuality. There was scandal and a court martial. Austen would have known all about sodomy in the Navy. Grab the smelling salts, if you please.[16]

Not everyone had such a supportive family. So while there were men like John Joyce who had a wealthy family to help him get back on his feet, there were countless men who had no such help. Many lost their lives. One of the most horrible witch hunts in early-modern Britain was the Mother Clap Trials.

## Mother Clap Trials

If your historical hero is bouncing from brothel to brothel in the 1720s, he's going to be very aware of the existence of gay brothels. Likewise, if your heroine owns a *molly house* (gay brothel), she's going to be very, very afraid.

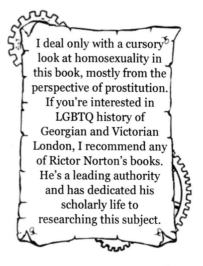

I deal only with a cursory[6] look at homosexuality in this book, mostly from the perspective of prostitution. If you're interested in LGBTQ history of Georgian and Victorian London, I recommend any of Rictor Norton's books. He's a leading authority and has dedicated his scholarly life to researching this subject.

Margaret Clap, commonly known as Mother Clap, ran a coffee house that was a front for a molly house. In Clap's case, she wasn't running a brothel in the traditional sense of the word. There were male prostitutes working out of her home, but mostly it was a gathering place for the gay community. She didn't care if they had sex at her house, and had set it up so that they could do so in private, if they wished.

She earned her income from her tenants and the drinks she served. Clap was well-known and, by all accounts, seemed well-liked[17]. Police constables converged on Margaret Clap's house in February, 1726 and imprisoned anyone present. Similar raids happened nearby to other molly houses. Agents collected evidence on well-known gay hangouts, including around St. Paul's Cathedral and Field Lane, where Mother Clap's coffee house was.[18]

## Elizabeth Canning
## (1734 – 1773)

On Jan 29 1753, Elizabeth Canning stumbled home half-naked, exhausted, and confused. She'd been missing four weeks and no one, not even Canning, knew exactly where she'd been.

She said she'd been kidnapped by gypsies and was locked in a bawdy-house. Was she locked in a bawdy house? Had she been kidnapped? Had something even worse happened to her? How did she know so much about specific parts of the interior of the house, yet know so little about other areas? There were endless inconsistencies in her story, but also some truths. After 260 years, scholars still do not know what exactly happened.

She had impeccable character before and after this event. If she was lying, which it seems she was, what on earth happened to her to make her think this option was a better one? How did she know about the size of the house and the rooms, the very nature of the inside of the brothel, and the freaking hayloft if she'd never been there?[13] There are books written about Canning: some call her a liar, some call her hysterical, and some believe Canning herself didn't even know what happened to her.

The first trial was on April 20, 1726 against Thomas Wright, who was charged with buggery against Thomas Newton. Newton testified against Wright: "the Prisoner had the Carnal Use of my Body at his own House[19]." Newton, however, was a male prostitute who had been blackmailed and threatened into giving up his friends and lovers. Wright was found guilty and sentenced to death.

Next up on the docket was Gabriel Lawrence, "indicted for feloniously committing with Thomas Newton" (yes, him again) "the heinous and detestable Sin of Sodomy[20]" at Mother Clap's house. Newton's testimony gave an account of Clap's house, including Sundays being her busiest day and having about 30-40 patrons a night and having beds in every room, just like in heterosexual brothels. Newton said he "suffer'd the Prisoner to commit the crime." Lawrence was convicted and sentenced to death.

William Griffin was next, indicted for committing sodomy with Thomas Newton. Griffin was apparently a lodger at the Clap's house for nearly two years. Again, Newton testified. Guilty. Death. Next.

And on went the witch-hunt. Two more men were tried, who were unconnected with Clap's establishment, but were most likely known in the gay community. George Kedear was found guilty and sentenced to death, though George Whytle was found not guilty. In these two men's cases, Edward Courtney provided the testimony as the man who had been "buggered".

Some of the trial records, beyond Clap's, mention Samuel Stevens. He was an undercover investigator and openly testified he'd spent plenty of time at various gay brothels. Investigating, of course. He occasionally backed up Newton's testimonies[21].

On May 9, 1726, the three men from Mother Clap's were executed together.

This wasn't the end, as Margaret Clap's trial began on July 11, 1726. Keeping a bawdy-house, even a homosexual one, was not a capital crime, so Clap's neck wasn't on the line. She still faced fines, imprisonment, and the pillory. At the same time, more of her customers were on trial, but for the lesser crime of intent, not for actually having committed sodomy. They likewise faced fines, imprisonment, and the pillory.

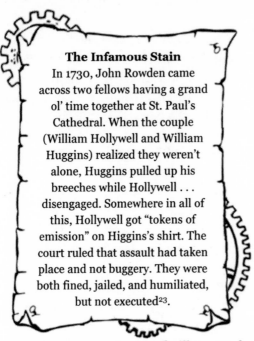

**The Infamous Stain**

In 1730, John Rowden came across two fellows having a grand ol' time together at St. Paul's Cathedral. When the couple (William Hollywell and William Huggins) realized they weren't alone, Huggins pulled up his breeches while Hollywell . . . disengaged. Somewhere in all of this, Hollywell got "tokens of emission" on Higgins's shirt. The court ruled that assault had taken place and not buggery. They were both fined, jailed, and humiliated, but not executed[23].

Samuel Stevens testified that he was at Margaret Clap's house and witnessed fifty men "making love to one another as they call'd it." The men would brag about their sexual exploits, he said, and Clap did nothing to stop it. In fact, she "appear'd wonderfully pleas'd with it.[22]" Guilty, guilty, guilty.

She was fined 13s.4p, two years prison, and pillory. We know nothing of her life once she went to prison.

## Boulton and Park Trial

The Mother Clap trials weren't the only example of persecuting gay men, but perhaps one of the more bloody examples. In 1871 London, the trial of Thomas Boulton and Frederick Park began. They were cross-dressers and suspected homosexuals. The death penalty for buggery had been abolished in 1861, so they "only" faced ten years to life in the penal system.

They were charged with "conspiring and inciting persons to commit an unnatural offence." Neither were convicted, since wearing women's clothing wasn't a crime and no one could prove they were having sex together[24].

## Cleveland Street Scandal

The Cleveland Street Scandal took place in 1889 at a male brothel on Cleveland Street. Charles Hammond, the owner, catered to an aristocratic clientele and the establishment was unknown to the police.

Then a fifteen-year-old telegraph boy, Charles Swinscow, was arrested and accused of stealing from work. They found a lot of money (for him) on him. He panicked and said he worked as a male prostitute at Hammond's. Then, the names of other boys came out, who were arrested.

The thing was the investigation brought up some interesting names of potential and actual clients. Colonels, Lords, Earls . . . and Prince Albert, the Duke of Clarence, second in line to the throne.

Awkward.

It appears that the authorities purposely dragged their feet, allowing a key figure (who would have pointed at the Duke) to flee England. However, the telegraph boys didn't get that privilege, being poor and all. They were all convicted and sentenced to several months of hard labour. The Duke of Clarence conveniently left on a tour of India during the trials.

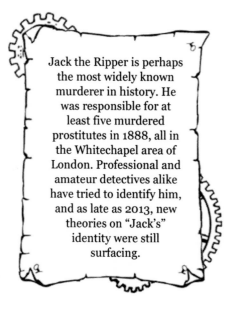

Jack the Ripper is perhaps the most widely known murderer in history. He was responsible for at least five murdered prostitutes in 1888, all in the Whitechapel area of London. Professional and amateur detectives alike have tried to identify him, and as late as 2013, new theories on "Jack's" identity were still surfacing.

Was the Duke a real client or not, and did the government purposely try to cover it up? Well, I suppose it all depends on how you view the evidence trail. I'll leave it up to you to find out for yourself. After all, that sounds like a great detective novel.

## Homosexual Cures

It wasn't until the 1880s that there were true attempts to cure homosexuality. Before then, legal and religious methods were often used. Imprisonment and death typically were considered the best cures. Religious figures recommended penance . . . or death. One man confessed his sexual inclinations to a priest, who advised he stop eating until the feelings went away. The man died of starvation.

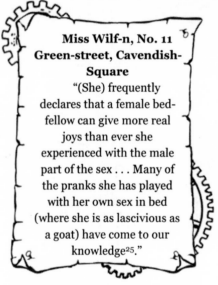

**Miss Wilf-n, No. 11 Green-street, Cavendish-Square**

"(She) frequently declares that a female bedfellow can give more real joys than ever she experienced with the male part of the sex . . . Many of the pranks she has played with her own sex in bed (where she is as lascivious as a goat) have come to our knowledge[25]."

The brothel cure was always popular, especially in Georgian times. A large amount of alcohol and an experienced prostitute was generally thought the best cure to get . . . a rise out of even the staunchest homosexual.

The ladies, sadly, were referred to their husbands. Sorry, girls. No brothels for you.[26]

## That Burning Feeling

As the saying went, "five minutes with Venus may mean a lifetime with Mercury.[27]" Venus was the popular and cheeky way writers referred to prostitutes, as they were in service to Venus, the Roman goddess of love. At the time, syphilis was treated with mercury.

Most venereal diseases were considered syphilis, even if the symptoms could be very different. The dose of mercury was all the same, too. Mercury made the body sweat, which medical understanding at the time thought restored the body's equilibrium. Mercury was (brace yourself) injected into one's urethra, rubbed on the skin, or coated into underpants and worn.

A side effect of advanced mercury poisoning is bad breath and black saliva. As it happens, black saliva was considered the key way to tell the mercury was working, so people were being way overdosed to get this "desired" effect. And the mercury did work in fighting syphilis; it just shortened your lifespan by decades.

Unfortunately, there were also other stories about how to get rid of infection. There were children admitted to lock houses for treatment; there was a theory that sex with a small child would cure a man. Pregnancy was also thought as the cure for women, as it transferred the illness from one host to another.

## Famous Players

Not all prostitutes were nameless, faceless women who performed sex acts in disgusting alleys. Some were celebrities, who lived the high life. Some ended up in bad circumstances, others in fabulous ones. But even those who had tragic ends, they lived grand lives. So this section is about four of the grandest: Sally Salisbury, Lavinia Fenton, Kitty Fischer, and Elizabeth Armistead.

Sally Salisbury (1692-1724) is the first of our celebrity sex workers and is most likely the inspiration for Hogarth's *Harlot's Progress*.

She was sent to apprentice with a milliner when she was nine years of age. She was accused of stealing some lace and was whipped for it. Nothing else is known about what happened to her then, but we see her again at sixteen. Someone wrote that Sally was charging half a crown for an hour of "her love; that being her usual price[28]."

Like many younger prostitutes, Sally had various protectors who were regulars. Protectors helped keep women out of the hands of cruel bawds and let them live a comfortable life. Sally was abandoned by her protector in 1709. At nineteen, she met the bawd Elizabeth Wisebourne who decided the Sally had the wit, personality, and beauty necessary to be more than just another common prostitute. She dressed Sally in finery and paraded her accordingly. Her prices also skyrocketed.

Sally's fame grew and she lived an independent life, something very few women in the early 18th century could claim for themselves. She had famous clients, including the future King George II. She hung out with the top quality of London at the peak of her popularity. Myths about her reputation, beauty, and amorous attentions grew.

She became pregnant. She got an abortion. She contracted venereal disease. She got a doctor. Sally refused to let anything stand in her way.

However, Sally's drinking, drug use, and perhaps her illness caused her self-control to slip. She stabbed a lover with a knife. As he clung to life, she was arrested to await trial. As with all celebrities, the gossip mill turned against her. Folks love to cheer the fall of the popular girl who thumbed her nose at all propriety.

Sally's trial was in April 1723. She was found guilty of assault and not attempted murder. She was fined £100 (a hefty sum) and sentenced to a year in prison[29].

Unfortunately, Sally never lived to make it out of Newgate prison. She died in 1724 with three months left in her sentence. It's not certain if she died of syphilis or "Gaol Fever" caused by prison conditions. Sally was a sad tale of a bright star who died out too early.

Though, in reading the stories told about Sally and the biographies written about her, I wonder if she would have seen it that way. She probably would have argued that life wasn't worth living if you didn't shine as bright as possible.

Most women weren't like Kitty Fisher (?-1767), who demanded 100 guineas a night. Most were working with bawdy-houses with most of their earnings going to the owners. Many of the lower street walkers made 1 shilling per sex act. That was still a lot of money, considering that was a week's rent in one of the slums.[30] Shortly before her death, Kitty left prostitution all together and married John Norris, the son of an MP and a grandson of an Admiral. She was well-liked, kind to the poor, and settled into domestic life. Sadly, she died a few months later.

Lavinia Fenton (1708-1760) was a child prostitute who became a popular actress. She caught the eye of Charles, Duke of Bolton, became his mistress, and bore him three children. When Bolton's wife died in 1751, he did the unexpected: he married his mistress. They lived together happily for nine years before her death.

When romance novels write about the Duke marrying a prostitute, they're actually writing about Lavinia's life.

But perhaps none were more talked about than courtesan and actress Elizabeth Armistead (1750-1842) who married politician Charles James Fox. Elizabeth had become the mistress to several of the aristocracy and it was through those social connections that she and Fox had become friends. After a decade of them knowing each other, she became his mistress and they married in secret in 1795.

It wasn't until 1802 that everyone found out their favourite (or most hated, depending on one's politics) politician had married his courtesan mistress several years before. It was a shock and much talked about, but society soon accepted her.

## Florence Nightingale (1820-1910) and Mary Seacole (1805-1881)

Florence Nightingale wanted to both be a nurse and to train nurses. She came from a rich family who didn't initially support her wanting a career in an unladylike profession. However, they eventually relented and she went to Germany to learn nursing.

During a cholera outbreak in London, Nightingale volunteered to oversee one of the hospitals and the nurses. When the Crimean War broke out, news reports detailed the suffering of injured troops. Nightingale was part of a group of women who went to help.

It was during the Crimean War that Nightingale cemented the role of the nurse. She returned to London in 1856 and pressured the government to look into military health care. In 1860, she opened a nursing school, changing the face of nursing forever[1].

Mary Seacole was a biracial woman who learned traditional nursing in Jamaica from her mother. She travelled widely and sought out modern medical information. In 1854, while in England, she approached the War Office and asked to be sent as an army nurse to the Crimea to help Nightingale, but was refused because of her race.

She used her own money and went to Turkey herself. There, she set up a hotel that provided food, lodgings, and care to British soldiers. Sometimes, she went to the front to help the soldiers, as Nightingale's hospital was further back. Seacole was awarded several medals for bravery[2].

# Chapter 11: Cleanliness Leads To Drunkenness

*"Slovenliness is no part of religion . . . Cleanliness is indeed next to godliness."*
-John Wesley, *On Dress: Sermon 88*

This was a challenging chapter to put together because there are still so many more things I could include, but haven't. I've only mentioned hospitals a few times up to now. Nothing about gin. Nothing about germs. I've skimmed over the risks of pregnancy. So this chapter is the hodgepodge excuse for me to a) talk about all of those topics and, more importantly, b) to say hodgepodge.

Hodgepodge.

Haberdashery.

I'll stop now.

Unless you're directly writing a steampunk-themed novel about germ research—please email if you do, I'm fascinated already—most of the information in this chapter isn't going to grace the pages of your own stories. That doesn't mean it's not important. Small things can creep into your works, such as a grandparent's disgust at seeing a

London smelled, especially in the summer time. In fact, in 1858, London smelled so bad that Parliament couldn't meet to discuss the stench and it was dubbed The Great Stink.

bottle of gin, or a daughter being scrubbed with caustic soap to keep the germs away.

## That's Icky

It's hard to imagine a world where we didn't know about germs. Germs are talked about more than the family cat. Don't put that in your mouth; it has germs. Don't touch that; it has germs. Germs, germs, germs.

The theory of humors and miasma dominated medical understanding until the Victorian age. A French chemist and biologist named Louis Pasteur proved germ theory. Many people didn't believe tiny organisms as small as bacteria could kill large creatures like people.

The Theory of Humors dominated Western Europe during the Middle Ages. The theory was that humans were made of four elements: blood, phlegm, yellow bile, and black bile. Sickness was caused by one of these being out of balance, causing anything from a bad mood to death. For a long time, meat was combined with spices like pepper and ginger, and vinegar was added to mustard and garlic sauces. This was not to cover up spoiled food, but rather an attempt to keep people well.

A British surgeon named Joseph Lister showed that sterilizing surgical instruments and cleaning wounds led to less death from infections. Lister's work was backed up by the results of Ignaz Semmelweis and Oliver Holmes, but hospitals continued to perform surgery without basic cleanliness. In fact, it was a point of pride to have a messy, unwashed surgical gown because it proved one's abilities and experience. Lister required his surgeons to wash their hands in carbolic acid solutions and the instruments were washed in this, too.

By the late Victorian age, people accepted that germs were everywhere and on everything. Their immediate reaction was to scrub every single thing and person within an inch of their lives. A lot of the folklore of cleanliness in the kitchen still applied. Scrubbing and salting down wooden tables before and after cutting meat for curing, for example, was a viable way to kill bacteria.

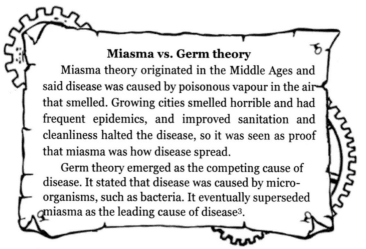

**Miasma vs. Germ theory**
Miasma theory originated in the Middle Ages and said disease was caused by poisonous vapour in the air that smelled. Growing cities smelled horrible and had frequent epidemics, and improved sanitation and cleanliness halted the disease, so it was seen as proof that miasma was how disease spread.
Germ theory emerged as the competing cause of disease. It stated that disease was caused by micro-organisms, such as bacteria. It eventually superseded miasma as the leading cause of disease[3].

But how people cleaned themselves changed. Before, there was a belief that getting water on one's pores opened them up to disease. Women would not need to worry about hot water. People disinfected their hands now. Carbolic acid was sold in soap form and its sharp smell meant that a person was clean.

Victorian girls looking for domestic work would do well to smell like carbolic soap. They'd have a sharp, hospital smell to them, which would have been seen as a positive. It was a sign that there were no dangerous germs on their bodies; it would increase their likelihood of finding and keeping employment.

It sounds strange, but we have the same relationship with hand sanitizer. There are some people who smell like hand sanitizer all of the time, especially in the workplace during cold and flu season. When the craze first began, every bus and public space smelled like alcohol. Carbolic soap was the Victorian equivalent to today's sanitizers.

Toothpaste (called dentifrice) also became more common, with many people making their own. After all, germs weren't just on your body, but inside it. Toothpaste helped clean those germs out.

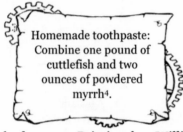

Homemade toothpaste: Combine one pound of cuttlefish and two ounces of powdered myrrh[4].

## Mother's Ruin

Gin became known as Mother's Ruin in the mid-18th century. Gin was a medicinal drink and fairly harmless, and had come to Britain when William of Orange took the throne during the Glorious Revolution. Later, when war with France broke out— as it was apt to happen—the British government put import taxes on spirits from elsewhere, which made English-produced spirits cheaper to purchase.

England already suffered from low cereal crop prices, the import taxes lowered the prices even more. Gin has a strong, juniper flavour that people mistakenly believe means the juniper is the main ingredient. In fact, gin's base is grain, and then it's flavoured with juniper berries. So, by about 1750, almost half of Britain's wheat harvest was going directly to making quite cheap gin. The effects of this turned gin drinking to a devastating social issue in the 18th century.

It's hard to understand how one drink could cause so much social ruin, so it's important to reflect on everything we've learned in this book so far. Georgian London was crowded, dark, and slum-ridden. People were hungry, cold, underemployed, and desperate. For the bulk of London's inhabitants, surviving the week was their only focus. The beer they typically drank wasn't going to get them drunk, just fill their bellies with bloat and carbs.

But gin could make them blind drunk and forget their problems.

Spirits were typically expensive, but gin was cheap. It cost a penny for a loaf of bread during the gin craze. That was the same price that someone could spend to get drunk off gin. Gin was everywhere. By the 1730s, there were anywhere from 6000-7000 gin houses or "dram houses" in London openly selling the stuff. It was also purchasable from street costermongers, grocers, barbers, and in brothels[5].

The amount of gin distilled and drank in London was staggering. In 1730, ten million gallons of gin were sold in London alone. By 1750, it was estimated that every fifteenth house in London was a dram house. Gin was everywhere.

It was being made in prisons, workhouses, even hospitals. Wheelbarrows filled with gin were pushed around the poorest areas. Parish nurses gave it to children to shut them up and over nine thousand children died directly because of gin in 1751 alone.[6] William Hogarth drew a satirical print called "Gin Lane" in 1751, where a woman lets her baby plunge to his death.

> "(S)hould the drinking this poison be continued at its present height during the next twenty years there will by that time be very few of the common people left to drink it."- Henry Fielding, *Enquiry into the causes of the late increase of robbery* (1751)

Even if a person wanted to get away from it, it was nigh impossible during the craze.

To make the gin even cheaper, it was being flavoured with anything cheap, including dangerous substances like turpentine. Turpentine could cause a host of issues, including kidney damage, when ingested. Sulphuric acid was also added, accounting for madness, low birth rates, and high death rates.

The rampant binge drinking and alcoholism, plus all of the social problems that come from excessive drinking, prompted public interest and concern. The outcry became too much for the government to ignore and they began to take action. The 1736 Gin Act taxed retail sales and instituted a £50 selling licence. Unfortunately, the reputable places went out of the business and the bootleggers thrived. Several more laws were passed, all aiming to fight the selling and consumption of gin.

The gin craze increased in pitch, so the Gin Act of 1751 was passed to combat the cheap prices. This and several poor wheat harvests caused an increase in food costs and a drop in wages. By 1757, no one could afford gin and the craze was finally dead.

A century later after the Gin Craze, Mayhew noted that the poor still drank more than his middle-class roots said was wise. He estimated that "heavy drinkers" spent 12s of every 20s they earned on beer and "entertainment." He didn't elaborate on what debauchery that entailed.

## Safe Sex Is Not So Safe

I have something shocking to share: people in Jane Austen's time had sex. Coitus. The bow chicka wow wow. The beast with two backs. Whatever you want to call it, they were doing it. And not with their spouses.

Venereal disease was rampant, especially syphilis. Condoms were used to help protect men against disease. They weren't generally used with one's wife, however, and were seen as a tool to prevent disease in a man and not much else. Besides, why else would you have sex with your wife if it wasn't to get her pregnant?

But there were plenty of ways to avoid pregnancy as the Victorian era steamed forward. With the development of inexpensive rubber came rubber condoms and the rubber cervical cap. The cervical cap put birth control solely in the discreet hands of the woman, a liberating notion for many. The sponge was well-known amongst upper class women.

Condoms were made out of sheep's intestines, soaked in water, and fastened around the man's base with a ribbon. When done, he washed the condom and allowed it to dry out again for reuse.

*Coitus interruptus* was another popular choice amongst those wanting family planning. As was douching with water mixed with either alum, vinegar, baking soda, or chloride[7]. So heroes like Mark shouldn't show their surprise at their lady friend stepping out of bed for a few minutes to "freshen up."

Women also had access to early forms of birth control medications in the guise of "female pills" for helping regulate a woman's menstrual cycle. They were, obviously, well-known to prevent and stop pregnancy. The pills were marketed for those suffering a "stoppage of the menses" and to stop "obstruction." Some products had notes warning that women wishing to be mothers not take the product, making it clear what the pills did[8].

These pills weren't filled with wholesome ingredients. While the typical abortifacient ingredients were used, such as pennyroyal, rue, and black cohash, they also might contain ingredients such as lobelia (similar to nicotine) and turpentine. Many women ingested these toxic materials into their bodies monthly as a form of contraception or "health tonic[9]."

## In the Family Way

I'm spoiled in Canada. There is a social safety net and labour laws that protect me if I become pregnant, injured, or ill. Here, new parents get about a year of what's called Employment Insurance (EI). The bulk of that time is sharable between the parents, too, and is about half of one's annual income. People like Martha and Mark had no such luxury.

Regency-era women gave birth to an average of six or seven babies in their lifetimes. Without access to proper and safe birth control methods, and with breastfeeding often not practical or allowed for working and upper-class women, this left many women having far more children than they could care for or even wanted.

The Georgians and Victorians brought us the concept of "laying in", where a very pregnant and new mother would be locked up in her room for a month to ensure she did not become sick and die. However, this was a luxury for the leisure class.

Working class women did not have that luxury (and, in some countries, still don't).

My mother often talks about how she gave birth to her eighth

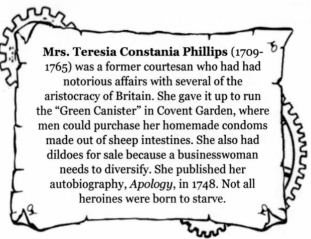

**Mrs. Teresia Constania Phillips** (1709-1765) was a former courtesan who had had notorious affairs with several of the aristocracy of Britain. She gave it up to run the "Green Canister" in Covent Garden, where men could purchase her homemade condoms made out of sheep intestines. She also had dildoes for sale because a businesswoman needs to diversify. She published her autobiography, *Apology*, in 1748. Not all heroines were born to starve.

child, and had seven others under the age of nine waiting for their dinner. She gave birth, cleaned herself up, and got to making meals since there was no time to lie around.

Working-class women worked as long as they physically could, though unmarried women did not have that luxury. They lot their jobs when found out. At least 5% of children were illegitimate during the Regency era, which rose to 7% in the early Victorian era, before falling back down. However, there was so much stigma attached to being an unwed mother that it's likely the rates were higher[10].

Some unwed women with savings would use services like this one offered in an 1803 ad[11]:

> PREGNANT LADIES, whose situations requires a temporary retirement, may be accommodated with an Apartment, in an airy situation, to Lye-in, agreeably to their circumstances, their infants put out to nurse, and taken care of. Tenderness, honour, and secrecy, have been the basis of this concern for many years.

The ad goes on to say they wouldn't take in women who didn't care about their reputation, or the reputation of the family taking them in. The service was designed for women who want to hide their sinful pregnancy, not flaunt it.

If Martha became pregnant, she might invent a sick relative and leave for half a year to stay with distant relations or even a lying-in service like in the ad. Then, she could return, sans pregnancy and carry on working. Or, return with her "cousin's" newborn, who was too sickly to care for the little one.

Or if Mark got a girl "in trouble" and didn't want to marry her, he might offer to pay to send her away to stay with some people who could look after her and try to protect her identity and reputation. While marriage would be the best circumstance, the trip would allow her the opportunity to take on a new identity, such as pretending to be a young widow,

The 19th century saw a number of family planning books for young, married couples. Francis Place (1823) wrote pamphlets for the working class. Richard Carlisle wrote *Every Woman's Book* (1826) and American Charles Knowlton wrote *Fruits of Philosophy* (1832).

whose husband died tragically at sea. Or she might embrace her single motherhood, spurn the naysayers and the judgmental eye, and continue to hold her head high.

Most women gave birth at home. The poorest women in London had access to what was called lying-in hospitals from the mid-1700s. These were charitable facilities that took these women, often young girls, in during their last month of pregnancy and let them remain for a short time after the baby was born.

The maternity hospitals, or lying-in hospitals as they were originally called, offered poor women supervision by a physician during birth. Unfortunately, the insanitary conditions of the doctors and instruments meant that the chance of developing infection and puerperal fever was high.

Pregnancy exhausted women, physically and emotionally,

plus was more likely to impoverish them. Husbands had full legal control over a wife's body; for some women, saying not tonight wasn't an option. Young girls who'd been raped or "seduced" (in my mind, there often isn't much of a difference between the two) risked their jobs and livelihoods if they became pregnant.

Pregnancy wasn't always a joyous event for women, especially for the poor, but also those who'd given birth to several children and weren't even out of their twenties. It was another mouth to feed, another disappointment, and another potentially fatal circumstance.

## What About Unwelcomed Pregnancy?

I've encountered a lot of interesting reactions to my fiction, and have received some fairly oddball comments and complaints. There isn't an author out there who hasn't at some point. Authors often say that you haven't really made it until someone takes the time to blog about how awful your book was. But, there is nothing like getting emails that make your jaw drop. For me, those emails are about abortion.

I've openly discussed in public and online reactions people have when I discuss historical abortion. It's a topic that brings out a lot of anger in people. Some people incorrectly believe that abortion is a modern invention. It isn't. Abortion has been happening for a very long time. So let's talk about the realities of pregnancy before abortion and baby drop off locations were legal.

While abortion wasn't legal, abortion happened and happened at all ranks; abortion wasn't only for poor, young women who'd been abandoned. Women of all ranks sought out abortions for many different reasons. Lady Clermont, a society lady and friend of the great Spencer family (the great Georgiana Cavendish and Diana "Lady Di" Spencer came from that branch) had an affair with an apothecary of all people. She had an abortion to cover it up.

Many foods and chemicals had known abortive qualities.

Women ingested ergot, rue, penny royal, tansy, and savin (juniper). Those who didn't have access to medications used wire or knives to perform their own abortions. Some women purposely threw themselves down flights of stairs or against chairs. More resorted to being punched repeatedly in the stomach. Women tightened corsets and punched themselves.

In 1875, Dr. Pye Chevasse wrote a book called Advice to a Wife, where he points out that a fetus was still alive before "quickening" (that is, when she could first feel her baby move inside her). Traditionally, quickening was when the baby was considered "alive" and a human being. Chevasse challenges this in his book: "The old-fashioned idea was that the child was not alive until a woman had quickened."

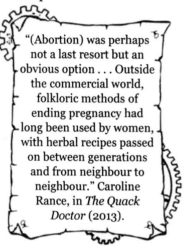

"(Abortion) was perhaps not a last resort but an obvious option . . . Outside the commercial world, folkloric methods of ending pregnancy had long been used by women, with herbal recipes passed on between generations and from neighbour to neighbour." Caroline Rance, in *The Quack Doctor* (2013).

Reading between the lines of Chevasse's words, women were choosing abortions up to the time of quickening. A woman might feel the baby moving inside her anywhere from 16 to 25 weeks, so if she were to make the choice, she'd traditionally seek out abortive measures before that time.

## Unwanted Children

There are a number of reasons why a woman might carry her unwanted child to term, including being too inexperienced and isolated to know until it was too late. This was probably common with young girls who'd been raped or had had sex without understanding exactly what they were getting themselves into.

A woman in desperate financial difficulties might deliberately become pregnant so that she could be a wet nurse and make a living. The newborn was dumped and she went on to earn money.

The *British Medical Journal* protested this and by 1872 the Infant Life Protection Bill was passed.

For women who carried their unwanted children to term, they could abandon the newborns in public places like a market or the church steps. That made the child the responsibility of the parish. Foundlings would be passed off to workhouses or boarded with poor women, but the mortality rates were high[12].

There were also places like the London Foundling Hospital, where mothers gave up their babies and children. Children were given a number and a scrap of fabric. That way, if the mother could ever come back and claim her child, she could prove the baby was hers by matching the fabric pieces together. Very few women ever came back to claim their children, but if they did, they just needed to show the matching piece of cloth.

There were always the baby-farmers. They charged, some upwards of £15, but they "adopted" children. Unfortunately, these children typically weren't cared for. As soon as the fee was paid (the fee obtained through a woman's savings, money from the child's father, or sex work), the child was dumped. The children weren't murdered; corpses were inconvenient. But nothing stopped these people from leaving the child in another town.

A child of six could earn their own living, so these women weren't likely to find real adoptive parents for their unwanted children in any case.[13]

# Hospitals

Hospitals have existed in various forms and under various mandates for a long time. Medieval Britain had hospitals, for example, though they weren't merely for treating the sick. They also offered temporary board and lodging for travellers. BBC *Sherlock* fans will recognize the name of St. Bartholomew's Hospital, which was a way station for travellers from at least the 15th century[14].

Eventually, the hospital transitioned into a place for the sick, injured, the infected, and so on. Specialized hospitals were cropping up by the Georgian period to deal with the various specific needs of the population. Military hospitals, such as Chelsea Hospital and Greenwich Hospital, were established to deal with the unique needs of the war wounded and veterans. Liverpool opened a school/hospital for the blind in 1791, in an attempt to help patients support themselves with various skills.

Hospitals relied on charitable donations and contributions, and didn't receive any government assistance well into the Victorian age. Hospitals were supposed to be for the sick, obviously, but even into the middle-Victorian age, some hospital officials used available space for their servants.

To be admitted, a patient had to fill out paperwork and attend a weekly admission triage. Though, the triage was more based on who you knew and not what was wrong with you. If admitted, patients were looked after by physicians and surgeons.

The Victorian age also saw even more specialized hospitals. By 1860, there were 66 specialist hospitals in London, treating various diseases such as TB, VD, and others. Though, a successful cure was rarely guaranteed and often seemed more the province of luck and divine intervention than anything doctors did.

Lock hospitals, such as the London Lock Hospital, were set up to treat venereal diseases.

Until germs were proved to exist and cause illness, doctors would be inspecting open sores with hands that might have just touched cholera, gonorrhoea, pneumonia, and a host of infections. That was where homecare excelled. Houses and a wife could be cleaner and safer than the physician who was being paid to treat the patient![15]

Of course, perhaps the most common hospitals from this period were the 19th century asylums. The madhouses. The asylum system was developed as "institutional solutions to mental and physical disabilities rather than the community and familial care of the past[16]." And Bethlem Royal Hospital, aka Bedlam, is today still the most recognized of them all.

And after a year at Bedlam, if patients weren't cured by chains, prayers, and isolation, they could be sent to St. Luke's hospital for life-long care . . . provided the patient had a wealthy enough relative to pay the weekly 5s (mid-18th century price) for your upkeep[17].

Private asylums were for-profit and the rules for admission were troubling. These private asylums became the perfect way to get rid of unwanted people without having to bother with the uncomfortable situation of a corpse. Husbands treated the asylums as personal dumping grounds for unwanted wives.

Parliament had to pass legislation in 1763 in an attempt to curb madhouses from being prisons for wives. In investigating, it came out that madhouses were used to confine people who were not lunatics. Physicians didn't confirm if a person was insane. No one was refused from these establishments, provided the fees were paid.

And those fees weren't cheap. Rates could vary even within an asylum, anywhere from £20 to £60 a year, and the fees determined the quality of diet and living quarters.

The laws didn't stop innocent, healthy women from being committed against their will. In 1772, a woman was forced into a madhouse by her husband. She only stayed for two days, since he felt guilty for having done it, but during her time she was chained and handcuffed. She insisted on rescuing a fellow-inmate, but the house refused. The woman brought the issue before a judge, who went down to visit the woman. He discovered she'd been there for two years and the circumstances were so deplorable that he'd not go back, not for £5000 in his pocket[18].

## Sir William Thomson, Lord Kelvin (1824-1907)

William Thomson was a Scottish mathematician and physicist. He was the son of a math professor and was publishing scientific papers by the age of sixteen. Thomson himself became a professor in natural philosophy in 1846, a position he kept for fifty years.

He studied and wrote about the theories related to heat, magnetism, light, and the age of the Earth. Thomson is also known for his contributions to thermodynamics, electromagnetic fields, and the modernization of physics. By the end of his life, he'd published over 600 scientific papers in his lifetime and was awarded dozens of patents for his work.

His concept of "absolute zero of temperature," introduced in 1848, became the basis for the Kelvin scale, which was named after him. The Kelvin temperature scale went on to become an international standard.

He also had a keen interest in hydrodynamics (the study of liquids in motion). Thomson also invented a tide predicting machine and improved the mariner's compass. He worked as the scientific adviser for laying telegraph cables across the Atlantic.

His contributions to science were recognized and he was knighted, raising him to the ranks of the peerage.

# Chapter 12: Point A to Point B and Inventions in Between

*"Steam and sail for certainty, but one day I believe a steamship could power itself across the ocean to America . . . I did not mean any ship or steam engines in existence today, Sirs, but projecting forward the improvements in efficiency we steam engineers have attained in the past ten years, I think the prospect to be anything but a subject for amused dismissal."*
*Lord Bond seemed to find difficulty in breathing. "We steam engineers . . . we . . . ? You must . . . certainly design me a steam yacht, my dear. I wait with . . . great anticipation to see your best work."*
-Roberta Stephenson to Lord Bond about the future of steamships (Christopher Hoare, *Steam and Stratagem*)

Now that we are nearing the end of this journey, you must allow me a moment to complain about the Industrial Revolution. I learned about the Industrial Revolution first in high school and was fascinated by it. When I went to university, I immediately clamped on to it and majored in British history.

There's a small problem with that: every other class I took for four years covered a) the cotton gin b) the Industrial Revolution. Around year 3, I hated both with a fervent passion and swore I'd never, ever, ever do anything with those two topics again.

Grumble.

The Industrial Revolution didn't start with one invention, in one town, by one dude. Instead, it was a series of technological breakthroughs that created stepping stones for those after it. It was a revolution in a true sense of the word, since Britain and many other countries went from rural-based agricultural towns and villages to an urban and industrialized country.

It's generally accepted that the revolution began in Britain in the late 1700s. The locomotive engine is the most widely recognized, and certainly the flashiest, feature of the Industrial Revolution, but it wasn't the only one.

## Textiles

The textile industry was transformed during this period. Clothing, linens, and the like were made at home. Raw materials were purchased from shops, but the end result came from homes.

The 1700s saw a huge movement in cotton and textiles. The spinning jenny and, later, the spinning mule reduced the amount of time and work hours necessary to produce yarn. Reducing the amount of time to get the yarn meant that there was more product to create textiles with.

Of course, one needed the raw material to make the yarn in the first place. Enter the cotton gin, because you can't talk about

An early example of a spinning jenny

the Industrial Revolution without this machine. Unfortunately.

The cotton gin was developed by an American named Eli Whitney in 1793. It separated the raw cotton fibre from the cotton seed. This had been done by hand traditionally; the cotton gin was meant as a major time saving device. It revolutionized cotton agricultural development in the American south, and cotton manufacturing in Britain.

Unfortunately, this became an out-of-control cycle that impacted both slavery and colonialism. The ever-increasing need for cheap cotton directly impacted the massive reliance on slavery in the United States. After the American Civil War, Britain still needed cheap cotton, so they turned their attention to exploiting India, which detrimentally impacted that country both in socioeconomic and political ways.[1]

# Agriculture

Agriculture saw a huge boom in the Industrial Revolution and it radically changed farming forever. The inventions of the mid to late Victorian era ushered in a "Golden Age" of farming.

Historically, farming had been practiced in a rotation. Basically, the same crop wasn't grown on the same field two years in a row; the fields would rotate through wheat, turnip, barley, and then clover or peas[2]. This allowed the soil to be constantly revitalized and helped prevent disease.

Farmers used rotted manure, compost, and bone meal to fertilize their crops, though they weren't exactly sure how this worked. They knew it did, but they didn't know the chemistry behind it.

Enter folks like Sir Humphrey Davy and Justus von Liebig who pioneered chemical development and soil analysis. Understanding what soil was composed of, what plants needed to grow, and how to add those nutrients to soil revolutionized farming.

Chemical fertilizers were developed and there were over a thousand fertilizer manufacturers in England and Wales by the

1870s. This gave the added benefit that a farmer could continue to grow cash crops without having to worry about soil depletion, though it did nothing for disease.

Improvements also came in the tools used on the farm.

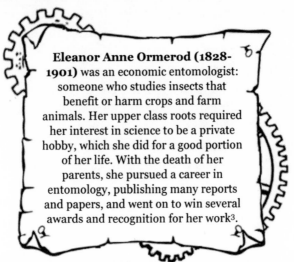

**Eleanor Anne Ormerod (1828-1901)** was an economic entomologist: someone who studies insects that benefit or harm crops and farm animals. Her upper class roots required her interest in science to be a private hobby, which she did for a good portion of her life. With the death of her parents, she pursued a career in entomology, publishing many reports and papers, and went on to win several awards and recognition for her work[3].

Farming traditionally needed the extensive help of labourers, including children, to weed, harvest, and seed. Harvesting grain crops required good weather, and lots of sharp scythes and sturdy backs to cut through the grasses. Women and children gathered up the bundles to let them dry. The work was arduous and backbreaking.

If you want to see how much work it was, I highly recommend you check out the documentary *Tales from the Green Valley*. They harvest their crops using the traditional methods and your back and hands will ache just watching them.

Machines such as threshers replaced the work of hundreds of men. Men used to work all winter helping thresh grain from the chaff. Now, a thresher could do it in under a week with just the help of a handful of workers.

This had a massive cost in turns of work availability. Agricultural labourers were increasingly unable to support themselves during harvest season and had to move to either London or the manufacturing centers in the north to find work.

An early example of a thrashing machine. It would be hooked up to horses or a steam engine to move the conveyor belt to thrash the wheat.

## Getting Around

For centuries, people and goods got around Britain by either ships or roads. Getting fresh items from the countryside, like milk, was extremely difficult because it often spoiled before it arrived. Getting fresh fish from the coast to the inland communities just wasn't going to happen in July if no one could get their hands on some ice.

Two of the largest engineering feats of the Industrial Revolution were the canal system and the railway.

Canals were necessary to move heavy loads across Britain. Coal, for example, had to be moved by horse teams and carts, and not enough could be moved great distances easily to meet the demands of growing factories. The canals were dug and provided an excellent way to transport heavy raw materials.

Most of the canals required a horse to pull the boats, but one horse could tug along a full-loaded boat whereas it would take about a dozen horses to do the same job on land.

This reduced expense in moving items like coal reduced their price. This meant that factories and homes alike benefitted from cheaper fuel costs.

Also, the canal system impacted agriculture. It allowed farmers to move items such as dairy and strawberries farther distances. Farmers near canals began to adjust their crops to meet the needs of consumers at the other end of the canals who were only too happy to purchase fresh farm food. People like Mark, with a little ready cash on hand, could get their hands on fresh strawberries days, even maybe a full week, earlier because the canals would bring the fresh produce straight from the country fields to the London carts.

Of course, I can't mention the Industrial Revolution without the railway system. I tried really hard to get out of mentioning it, in fact. Lazy writers unite, am I right?

The period from horse-drawn trains to a massive rail network happened in only half a century. It was like those of us born in the 70s who saw the rise of personal computers and the development of the internet, back in the good ol' days when you could look up how to build bombs on Gopher.

Note to the Mounties: I never did this. Please don't arrest me.

The first working steam locomotive engine was built by Richard Trevithick for his iron works company in Wales in 1804. By 1811, John Blenkinsop invented a steam engine with cogs. This gave his engine more grip.

Around this time, George Stephenson (1781-1848) was

George Stephenson's Rocket Locomotive

becoming interested in engines and trains. As a youth, he worked in a coalmine with his father. He managed the engines used at the mine and eventually created his own in 1814.

In 1821, Stephenson went on to become the engineer for the construction of the railing from Stockton to Darlington. It opened in 1825 and was the first public railway. He then went on to work on the Liverpool-Manchester line. Railway owners staged a competition to see which engine was best for pulling large loads, and Stephenson's "Rocket" locomotive was the winner.

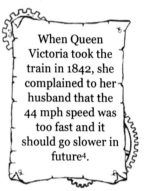

When Queen Victoria took the train in 1842, she complained to her husband that the 44 mph speed was too fast and it should go slower in future[4].

Railway mania took off. Fifty-four rail lines were approved between 1825 and 1835. In the one year between 1836 and 1837, Parliament approved thirty-nine lines! By the close of the century, Britain had laid over twenty thousand miles of rail track.

Like the canals, the railway provided better access to goods across Britain and at a cheaper price. Rail travel quickly came to be about half the cost of coach travel, and could carry perishables such as fresh fish inland. Soon, some cars were turned into ice boxes to transport perishables in the hot months.

The rail also changed how people worked. For centuries, people lived near where they worked. They had to. The railway changed this, by allowing people to live outside the city and commute.

Consider the impact that made on families and societies. People had to live near where they worked. Now, they could just hop on a train and live wherever they wanted. They could escape the city, or at least escape the slums. If Martha's mistress moved to the countryside, Martha might make it home every year or two for a visit. With trains, Martha could make a trip down to London for the weekend.

In 1844, Prime Minister Gladstone required train companies to offer a cheap ticket in third class that only charged 1d per mile for the working class who commuted. Soon, weekly tickets were purchasable for those who commuted to London every day.

The next time you're caught in traffic during rush hour, blame trains. It's all their fault.

## Luddites Don't Use Smartphones

Not everyone was peachy keen on all this newfangled technology. Today, anyone without a smartphone and a PVR is called a Luddite. The term these days is "simultaneously a declaration of ineptitude and a badge of honour[5]." The original Luddites weren't declaring themselves inept. They were fighting the loss of their livelihoods.

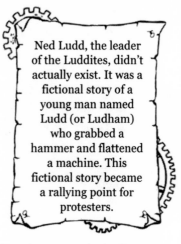

Ned Ludd, the leader of the Luddites, didn't actually exist. It was a fictional story of a young man named Ludd (or Ludham) who grabbed a hammer and flattened a machine. This fictional story became a rallying point for protesters.

The Luddite and the machine smashers can be traced to March 11, 1811 in Nottingham. British troops were called in to break up protesters who were demanding more work and better wages. The workers smashed textile machinery that night. The attacks spread in waves across the area. The government moved thousands of soldiers into the manufacturing districts and passed a law making machine breaking a capital offense.

The Luddites weren't actually as threatening as the government thought they were, nor were they planning a mass destruction of technology and advancement. There were some deaths, though there weren't mass civil riots and certainly the country wasn't under any real threat of an uprising.

Luddites were objecting to machines that replaced them. One of the biggest ones was a knitting machine that helped the textile industry grow. Jobs and employment was shifted from one area to another.

During the Industrial Revolution, workers were being displaced by machines. They were fine with machines, but not with factory owners who used the machines to create substandard labour situations and low-quality products. They wanted people to run the machines to be trained and paid living wages.

Thank heavens we don't have to worry about this today.

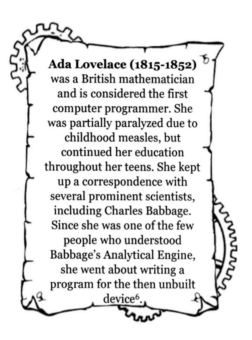

**Ada Lovelace (1815-1852)** was a British mathematician and is considered the first computer programmer. She was partially paralyzed due to childhood measles, but continued her education throughout her teens. She kept up a correspondence with several prominent scientists, including Charles Babbage. Since she was one of the few people who understood Babbage's Analytical Engine, she went about writing a program for the then unbuilt device[6].

## Chalres Babbage
## (1791 – 1871)

Babbage was born to a wealthy family, though a string of childhood illnesses put him in and out of school. He eventually made it to Cambridge, where he and his friends formed the Analytical Society for the mathematically-inclined.

Complex calculations had a lot of errors, due to human mistakes. Babbage wanted to remove the human component. His Difference Engine was designed to calculate logarithms and other mathematical functions using a system of cogs and gear wheels, and presented a paper on it in 1822.

He was given a government grant to construct the machine in 1823. It was a massive undertaking, as each cog and wheel had to be made by hand. He had to take a break in 1827 due to losing his wife, father, and son in the same year. The machine continued to get funding, even though there were cries that it was a waste of money. The machine wasn't finished by 1842 after a total investment of £23000 and the project was officially abandoned by the government.

However, Babbage continued working on improving his original design. He tried to create a machine between 1833 and 1842 to be programmable to do any calculation. During this time, Ada Lovelace began her lifelong correspondence and work relationship with Babbage. Baggage won awards and medals for his contributions to math, and was a professor at Cambridge. He wrote several scientific papers and was well-respected in his field.

He designed a second Difference Engine in the 1840s, though it wasn't built for another two centuries. The London Science Museum built his Difference Engine, completed in 1991. It worked perfectly.

# And So It Ends

*It was the best of times, it was the worst of times . . .*
-Charles Dickens, *A Tale of Two Cities*

It took us some time, but we've made it to the end. It's been a fun stroll through two popular British time periods. I'm disappointed that I had to leave so much out, and amazed I managed to fit so much in. There were a lot of tough choices in what made the cut or not, and all of those decisions were based on what I thought all of you would most want or need. I hope I've made the right decisions and have helped put you on the path of lots of questions.

We've covered a lot of history in this book. We've looked at the everyday lives of the poor and middle class, including where they lived and what they ate. We explored so many different occupations and careers, and the struggles those people endured.

At the beginning of this book, I talked about the myths I wanted to address.

- *Non-white people can't be in Regency novels.*
- *Slavery didn't exist in Britain.*
- *Slavery did exist, but it was over by the time Jane Austen was born.*
- *Women weren't allowed to work "back then."*
- *What I would give to live in Regency times; it was such a better time.*

I like to think that not only did I address those common myths, but that I trampled all over the fifth one. Most of us would have been the lower ranks. A few of us would have been in the middle class. Out of everyone who reads this book, chances are only one or two of us would have managed to break the glass ceiling and live in Lizzy Bennet's world, let alone Mr. Darcy's.

I hope that I've given you the right tools to look at your own manuscripts and find new and interesting ways to bring life and authenticity to your stories. If I've done my job, you'll be diving into the bibliography and ordering many of those books for your own reading.

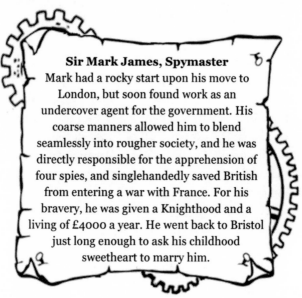

**Sir Mark James, Spymaster**
Mark had a rocky start upon his move to London, but soon found work as an undercover agent for the government. His coarse manners allowed him to blend seamlessly into rougher society, and he was directly responsible for the apprehension of four spies, and singlehandedly saved British from entering a war with France. For his bravery, he was given a Knighthood and a living of £4000 a year. He went back to Bristol just long enough to ask his childhood sweetheart to marry him.

As ever, I wish I could have done more. There's practically no mention of clothes anywhere in this book, and I really, really, really love clothes from this era. I didn't have the opportunity to explore the rural communities that surrounded London, and the very different lives that farmers and agricultural labourers lived. I'd have loved to take Martha and Mark to Scotland and Ireland, or maybe to the different British colonies to learn about the lasting scars of colonization.

Oh, and a full chapter on pistols, swords, muskets, and rifles. That would have been a lot of agonizing fun.

I feel a bit empty for not having had the space to tell you some of the stories I've read. Eight-year-old girls proudly declaring they were grown up and earning a liveable wage on their own. Twelve-year-old boys pimping out their girlfriends to bring in some spare change because they were both orphans and living on the streets. Sixteen-year-old boys proudly declaring they make enough money that their mothers can stay home and cook for them, instead of working out in the weather.

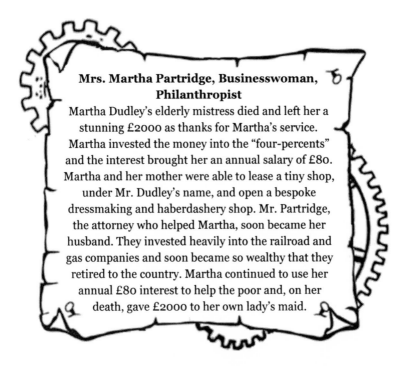

**Mrs. Martha Partridge, Businesswoman, Philanthropist**
Martha Dudley's elderly mistress died and left her a stunning £2000 as thanks for Martha's service. Martha invested the money into the "four-percents" and the interest brought her an annual salary of £80. Martha and her mother were able to lease a tiny shop, under Mr. Dudley's name, and open a bespoke dressmaking and haberdashery shop. Mr. Partridge, the attorney who helped Martha, soon became her husband. They invested heavily into the railroad and gas companies and soon became so wealthy that they retired to the country. Martha continued to use her annual £80 interest to help the poor and, on her death, gave £2000 to her own lady's maid.

But perhaps not addressing these issues gives you the opportunity to explore those themes on your own. *Hustlers, Harlots, and Heroes* is a basic guide, a whirlwind tour of a massive, huge period of social, political, and economic upheaval. There is no possible way to properly address all of the themes in one book.

If you're looking for more reading material and don't know where to start, I recommend starting with the bibliography. There are primary sources written by people of the period, and secondary sources by experts in their field. I've listed books by people who lived in the eras, and by people who have dedicated their lives to study the eras. I'm sure you'll enjoy what they have to say.

But where to go from here? One doesn't want to fill up their manuscripts with endless prattling about useless facts that distract from the heroine's vital mission for Horse Guards behind French lines. It's okay that the majority of the facts and figures in this book will never end up in your novels. Moderation is the key.

I recommend a light hand when adding in random bits of research. The goal is to never lose sight of the goal: entertaining readers. Keep them interested. Keep them hanging on your every word. And try to get everything right so that they don't email you two hours after your book launches pointing out an error.

And despite my frantic, sobbing calls to my friends, I've enjoyed writing this adventure. It's been a great time sitting at my desk with forty books piled on it and another 20 open on my laptop, just reading and taking notes. Cross-referencing. Digging deeper. It was also emotionally draining at times, reading story after story about young teenage girls who were forced to turn to prostitution for various reasons. It was painful to read Old Bailey manuscripts of gay men being executed for having consensual sex. I felt gross for the household waste I have, as I read about children standing in the Thames, snow collecting on their bare hands, as they picked up pieces of coal.

If this book taught me anything, it's that I am so grateful for the era in which I was born.

# Glossary of Common Terms

**Antimacassar**: Dollies on armchairs and sofas to protect the fabric from the macassar oil worn in men's hair.

**Apoplexy**: A stroke.

**Apothecary**: The lowest rank amongst medical men due to them being in "trade." They sold drugs, occasionally made house calls, and gave medical advice.

**Aristocracy**: It was frequently used to identify a member of the peerage, but was also applied at times to very wealthy men without title.

**Assizes**: In towns outside of London, justices of the peace met at quarter sessions to deal with crimes. They didn't deal with serious crimes, like murder and other capital crimes.

**Bagman**: Travelling salesman.

**Bawd**: A woman who procures prostitutes, including luring young girls.

**Bawdy house**: A brothel.

**Bob**: 1 shilling coin.

**Buck**: A debauchee.

**Buggery**: An interchangeable word for sodomy.

**Bully**: A man who protects prostitutes, similar to a bouncer.

**Bunter**: A destitute prostitute.

**Candlemas**: February 2

**Cholera**: Caused by a bacteria that lives in the intestine and is excreted in human waste. Symptoms include nausea, dizziness, vomiting, and diarrhea. Then followed by cramps, burning feeling, thirst, and often death within twenty-four hours of the symptoms showing up.

**Commerce**: An old form of poker.

**Clap**: A venereal disease, usually gonorrhea.

**Consumption**: Tuberculosis of the lungs.

**Copper**: 1 penny (pence) coin.

**Crown**: A coin worth five shillings. It was made from silver.

**Curate**: Typically a young man who has been recently ordered, he helped perform the duties of a clergyman. He might even be required to do all of the duties, but might only make £50 per year (early 19th century). They made up nearly half of the clergymen in England in the early 1800s. Curates were socially gentlemen, but were often treated as working class, since they were so poor.

**Dissenter**: Someone who did not follow the Church of England belief system. They might be Puritans, Unitarians, Quakers, Baptists, or a host of other groups that have broken off from the main Anglican faith.

**Dripping**: The fat that comes from roasted meat.

**Faro**: Players bet on the order in which cards will turn up when dealt off the bottom of a deck. A machine with a spring in it popped up the cards.

**Farthing**: A copper or bronze coin worth one-quarter of a penny.

**The Fleet**: London's main debtor's prison.

**The Game of Flatts**: Slang for lesbianism.

**Florin**: A silver coin worth two shillings.

**Forcemeat**: A meat-based stuffing, where meat is pounded together with vegetables and thickened with egg or breadcrumbs. It can be formed into patties, balls, sausage, or just formed into a casserole.

**Gaol Fever**: Typhus. It was common in prisons, where lice could spread between people.

**Gentoo**: An Indian who isn't a Muslim (i.e. a Hindu).

**Glorious Revolution of 1688-1699**: This revolution replaced the catholic King James, the reigning king, with his protestant daughter, Mary, and her husband, William of Orange. Some perspectives focus on it being a bloodless revolution in Britain, others focus on the bloodshed that was experienced in Ireland and Scotland. The revolution was as religious as it was political.

**Gout**: Common amongst the upper-class because of the abundance of wine and meat they ate. It caused a swelling in the joints, especially in the feet and big toes.

**Great Stink**: London was hot in 1858 and the Thames's water level fell. The new flush toilets had been dumping directly into the Thames, causing the river to deposit all manner of feces and garbage on its banks, which rotted and stank. This water was also being used by water companies and being drank by ordinary Londoners. It wasn't until the rain returned that the stink went away. Plans were then drawn up to deal with the sewer system and to prevent this from happening again.

**Guano**: A natural fertilizer from Peru. It was the sea-fowl droppings that had accumulated on cliffsides. It became popular in England once its chemical makeup and benefit to crops was understood. It became a major trade material between Peru and England between 1850 and 1870.

**Guinea**: Originally, this was worth one pound sterling (20 shillings), but eventually became worth 21 shillings due to the cost of gold. Guineas were considered more gentlemanly than a pound. You paid your servants and trades in pounds, but paid your artists and poets in guineas.

**Guy Fawkes Day**: November 5.

**Halfpenny**: A copper or bronze coin worth one-half of a penny. It was pronounced "haypenny" and not half-penny.

**Hard-ups**: Cigar-end, picked up by a street-picker. They were dried and sold as tobacco to the very poor.

**King's Bench Prison**: The southward-based prison generally used for holdings debtors and those guilty of libel.

**The Lock Hospital**: A hospital for the cure of VD. Founded in 1746.

**Macaroni**: A "foppishly" or silly dressed man.

**Macassar oil**: Conditioning oil used by Victorian men made from coconut and/or palm oil, ylang-ylang oil, and other fragrant oils.

**The Marshalsea**: Southward-based prison mainly used to house debtors to the 18<sup>th</sup> century

**Miasma theory**: Diseases such as cholera were spread by noxious air. This was the prevalent medical theory for contagious, infectious diseases until germs were discovered and accepted into medical understanding.

**Michealmas**: September 29 (A Quarter Day).

**Midsummer**: June 24.

**Molly house**: A brothel for gay and cross-dressing men to hang out and find sexual partners.

**Moorman**: This has two different meanings, depending upon the context. First, the Moors were the Muslim inhabitants of North Africa, the Iberian Peninsula, Sicily, and Malta. Secondly, the term Moor is used at times in a boarder sense to encompass Muslims born in the Middle East or Africa.

**Navvies**: The men who built the railway. At the peak of Railway Mania, 1 in 100 Britons worked as a navvy.

**Negus**: A hot drink made with water, port, sugar, and spices.

**Newgate**: London's chief prison where its most dangerous felons were held.

**Pimp**: A man who brings prostitutes and customers together.

**Potash**: Potash is a rich source of potassium that was typically found in wood ash. It wasn't widely available because it required burning wood and processing the ash. However, the Prussians in 1859 accidentally discovered a huge deposit while mining for salt and a large amount of it was purchased by British farmers for their fields.

**Pox**: Syphilis.

**Quarter Day**: Three-month periods of the year where rents were due, servants were hired for terms of labour, etc.

**Queer Cull**: A customer who favours anal intercourse.

**Quid**: A paper pound note.

**Rake**: A lewd debauched man who took advantage of women.

**Slavey**: A female domestic general servant, such as a maid-of-all-work.

**Sodomy**: Typically referred to sexual intercourse between two men, but was defined as any unnatural sexual act that was undertaken for pleasure and could not lead to procreation. A law was passed in 1533 making anal sex (buggery) illegal.

**Sovereign**: A pound in coin form.

**Speculation**: A round game where you ante up a set amount and the dealer anteing up double. Each player gets their cards until someone has a higher card than the trump. He may sell it. The holder with the highest trump wins.

**Street Arabs**: Homeless street children.

**Thruppence**: A three-penny coin.

**Tuppence**: A two-penny coin.

**Typhus**: Typhus is a different disease than typhoid fever; they are caused by different bacteria. Infected insects, such as lice, spread it to humans. Without antibiotics, typhus has a high death rate.

**Waltz**: A popular dance in Europe that was eventually allowed in Britain.

**White soup**: There are several version of white soup in period recipe books. Made from boiled broth (the "jelly" sediment when cooled), almonds, bread, thick cream, and spices. Macaroni or vermicelli could be optionally added, as in Rundell's (1833) recipe.

# Timeline of Events

|  |  |  |
|---|---|---|
| | 1714 | George I made king |
| George II made king | 1727 | |
| | 1746 | Jacobites are defeated |
| George III made king | 1760 | |
| | 1772 | Somerset case |
| American War of Independence begins | 1775 | |
| | 1781 | Zong Massacre |
| First convict fleet to Australia | 1787 | |
| | 1789 | French revolution begins Olaudah Equiano publishes autobiography |
| Britain goes to war with France | 1793 | |
| | 1803 | Napoleonic Wars begin |
| Battle of Trafalgar | 1805 | |
| | 1807 | Britain abolishes the slave trade |
| British West Africa Squadron is formed to stop slave trade | 1808 | |
| | 1811 | Regency of Prince of Wales begins Luddites begin attacks |
| War of 1812 starts | 1812 | |
| | 1813 | *Pride and Prejudice* is published |
| Stephenson demonstrates 1st steam engine | 1814 | |
| | 1815 | The Battle of Waterloo |
| *Frankenstein* published First human blood transfusion | 1818 | |
| | 1820 | George IV made king |
| World's first steam locomotive passenger service begins | 1825 | |

|  |  |  |
|---|---|---|
| 1901 | | Edward VII made king |
| 1900 | Boxer Rebellion | |
| 1899 | | Second Boer War Begins |
| 1897 | Women's suffrage movement gains momentum | |
| 1892 | | Dadabhai Naoroji is the 1st Asian MP elected |
| 1888 | Jack the Ripper's first victim | |
| 1883 | | Married women obtain right to acquire property |
| 1881 | First home to use electric light | |
| 1880 | | School is compulsory for children under 10 / First Boer War begins |
| 1879 | Anglo-Zulu War | |
| 1876 | | 1st telephone call |
| 1869 | Suez Canal opens | |
| 1865 | | *Alice in Wonderland* published |
| 1861 | Mrs. Beeton's *Household Management* is published | Britain's 1st female doctor qualifies |
| 1859 | | *On the Origin of Species* is published |
| 1847 | *Jane Eyre* published / Soyer develops soup kitchen | |
| 1845 | | Irish potato famine begins |
| 1840 | Vaccinations are introduced | |
| 1837 | | Victoria made queen |
| 1834 | New Poor Law was passed | |
| 1833 | | Slavery is abolished in British empire |
| 1830 | William IV made king | |

# Endnotes

Since this is a very general work, it was also impossible to narrow most facts presented to any one book, website, or documentary. I didn't want to turn people off by having streams of reference notes. I've opted to keep this book as general as possible; however, I still include references for anywhere that I've clearly quoted (either directly or paraphrased). Also, if there is only one major source for that information, I've included a reference to the source material.

Chapter 1
1   Andrew August, *Poor Women's Lives: Gender, Work, and Poverty in Late-Victorian London* (London: Associated University Press Inc, 1999), 20.
2   Liza Picard, *Victorian London: The Life of a City 1840-1870* (London: Orion Books Ltd, 2005), 83.
3   Roy Adkins and Lesley Adkins, *Jane Austen's England* (New York: Penguin Group (USA), 2013), Kindle edition.
4   Picard, *Victorian London*, 65.
5   Liza Picard, *Dr. Johnson's London: Life in London 1740-1770* (Great Britain: Weidenfeld & Nicolson. 2000), 61.
6   Peter Higginbotham, *Workhouses of the Midlands* (Great Britain: The History Press, 2009), 15.
7   Ruth Goodman, *How to be a Victorian* (London: Penguin Books Ltd. 2013), Kobo edition.

Chapter 2
1   Dan Cruickshank, *London's Sinful Secret: The Bawdy History of Very Public Passions of London's Georgian Age* (New York: St. Martin's Press, 2009) Kobo edition.
2   August, 23.
3   August, 65.

4   Picard, *Victorian London*, 71.
5   Rebecca Probert, "Living in Sin," *BBC History Magazine*, October 2012, 40-43.
6   Henry Mayhew, *London Labour and the London Poor*, Vol. 1-4. 1861. Digitized by Google Books.
7   Old Bailey Proceedings Online (www.oldbaileyonline.org, version 7.0, 02 February 2014), December 1795, trial of ANN TRACEY PETER TRACEY MARY BROWN (t17951202-38).
8   Old Bailey Proceedings Online (www.oldbaileyonline.org, version 7.0, 10 December 2013), September 1767, trial of James Brownrigg Elizabeth his wife John their son (t17670909-1).
9   Goodman, *How to be a Victorian,* Kobo edition.
10  Old Bailey Proceedings Online (www.oldbaileyonline.org, version 7.0, 02 February 2014), February 1746, trial of Francis Otter (t17460226-7).
11  Judith L. Newton et al, *Sex and Class in Women's history* (Great Britain: The Thetford Press Ltd, 1983), 137.
12  Newton, et al., 139.
13  Lucy Worsley, *If These Walls Could Talk* (New York: Bloomsbury, 2011), 75.
14  Amanda Vickery, *Radio 4's A History of Private Life*. AudioGo Ltd, 2010. Audiobook. Episode 16
15  Newton, *et al*, 115.
16  Charles Upchurch, *Before Wilde: Sex Between Men in Britain's Age of Reform*. (California: University of California Press, 2009), 4.
17  Vickery, *A History of Private Life (audio)*. Episode 16.

Chapter 3
1   Broomfield, Andrea. *Food and Cooking in Victorian England*. (Westpost, CT: Praeger Publishers, 2007), 25, 26.
2   Broomfield; 25.
3   Broomfield; 54.
4   Broomfield; 53.
5   Picard. *Dr. Johnson's London*, 64.
6   Goodman, *How to be a Victorian,* Kobo edition.
7   Peter Higginbotham. "The Workhouse" <http://www.workhouses.org.uk/life/food.shtml Consulted 16 September 2013.
8   Higginbotham, *Midlands*, 21.

Chapter 4
1   Picard, *Dr. Johnson's London*, 58-59.
2   The National Archives. <http://www.nationalarchives.gov.uk/education/lesson08.htm> Accessed June 27, 2013.
3   Picard, *Victorian London*, 75.
4   Picard, *Dr. Johnson's London*, 65.

Chapter 5
1   Picard, *Victorian London*, 97.
2   National Geographic. National Geographic Concise History of Science

and Invention: An Illustrated Time Line. (USA: National Geographic, 2009), 181.

3   Amanda Foreman, *The Duchess* (HarperCollins Publishers, 2008), Kobo Edition.

4   Lucy Inglis (2013-09-05). *Georgian London: Into the Streets* (Kindle Locations 4221-4222). (Penguin Books Ltd.), Kindle Edition.

5   The Royal Naval Museum. <http://www.royalnavalmuseum.org/info_sheet_impressment.htm> Accessed July 2, 2013

6   The War of 1812. http://www.warof1812.ca/food.htm, accessed June 5, 2012. The Discriminating General: 1995.

Chapter 6

1   http://www.amanda-foreman.com/PDFS/The_Times_How_do_you_solve_a_problem_like_Georgiana.pdf

2   Newton et al., 24.

3   A. N. Wilson. *The Victorians*. (New York: W. W. Norton, 2003), 318.

4   Vickery, *A History of Private Life (audio)*. Episode 10.

5   Jeremy Musson. *Up and Down Stairs.* (Great Britain: John Murray, 2009), Kobo edition.

6   M. Radcliffe, *A Modern System of Domestic Cookery* 1823. Digitized by Google Books.

7   Isabella Beeton. *The Book of Household Management*, 1861. Digitized by Project Gutenberg.

8   Beeton, Project Gutenberg edition.

9   Beeton, Project Gutenberg edition.

10  Worsley, 14.

11  Daniel Pool, *What Jane Austen Ate and Charles Dickens Knew* (New York Touchstone, 1993), 224.

12  Goodman, *How to be a Victorian*, Kobo edition.

13  Roy Adkins and Lesley Adkins, *Jane Austen's England* (Penguin Group US), Kindle Edition, 64.

14  Worsley, 31.

15  Foreman, Kobo edition.

16  Worsley, 35.

17  Musson, Kobo edition

18  Beeton, Project Gutenberg.

19  Beeton, Project Gutenberg.

20  Beeton, Project Gutenberg.

21  Musson, Kobo edition.

22  Pool, 223.

23  Picard, *Victorian*, 127.

24  John Henry Walsh, *A Manual of Domestic Economy* (London: G. Routledge & Co, 1856), Digitized by Google Books.

25  Walsh, Google Books.

Chapter 7

1   Picard, *Victorian,* 121.

2   Musson, Kobo edition.

3   Beeton, Project Gutenberg.
4   Maria Eliza Rundell, *A New System of Domestic Cookery* London: J. Murray, 1833. Digitized by Google Books.
5   Rundell, Google Books.
6   Rundell, Google Books.
7   Worsley, 14.
8   Radcliffe, Google Books.
9   Radcliffe, Google Books.
10  Chris Bowlby. "Changing Times: There's more to domestic service than Downton Abbey." BBC History Magazine. Oct 2012

Chapter 8
1   Mayhew, Google Books.
2   Mayhew, Google Books.
3   Picard, *Dr. Johnson's*, 10.
4   Picard, *Dr. Johnson's*, 15.
5   Picard, *Victorian London*, 72.
6   Pool, 238.
7   Pool, 239.
8   William Pybus, *A Manual of Useful Knowledge* (London: 1810), Digitized by Google Books.
9   Goodman, *How to be a Good Victorian*, Kobo edition.
10  Pool, 232.
11  Spitalfields Life. < http://spitalfieldslife.com/2010/09/29/the-life-of-a-mudlark-1861/ > Accessed November 20, 2013.
12  Mayhew, Google Books.
13  Mayhew, Google Books.
14  Vickery, (audio) Episode 5.
15  Picard, *Dr. Johnson*, 133.
16  Worsley, 75.
17  Picard, *Dr. Johnson*, 213.
18  August, 96.

Chapter 9
1   Fryer, 107.
2   Sukhdev Sandhu. < http://www.bbc.co.uk/history/british/empire_seapower/black_britons_01.shtml > August 2, 2013.
3   Benson, 4.
4   Fryer, 75, 79.
5   Fryer, 75, 79.
6   Barbara Wells Sarudy. < http://bjws.blogspot.ca/2013/10/hunting-fowling-shooting-in-18c-british.html > Accessed January 16, 2014.
7   Fryer, 17.
8   Fryer, 60.
9   There are various spellings for James Somerset and Charles Stewart.
10  The National Archives. < http://www.nationalarchives.gov.uk/pathways/blackhistory/rights/slave_free.htm > October, 28, 2013.
11  Fryer, 124.

12  There is some debate if these are the exact words of Mansfield, as only some of the court reporters recorded it. However, it's taken that these words were uttered at some point, and are often used as the famous words of the case, no matter who said them in the end.

13  David Dabydeen. BBC History. < http://www.bbc.co.uk/history/british/abolition/africans_in_art_galle ry_03.shtml >. Accessed December 2, 2013.

14  Fryer, 126.

15  Fryer, 129.

16  Fryer, 129.

17  William Cotter. *The Somerset Case and the Abolition of Slavery in England.* )Oxford: The Historical Association, 1994), PDF: > http://equianosworld.tubmaninstitute.ca/sites/equianosworld.tubman institute.ca/ files/Cotter%20Somerset%20Case.pdf>, 31.

18  Stephen Usherwood. "The Black Must Be Discharged," in History Today. < http://www.historytoday.com/stephen-usherwood/black-must-be-discharged-abolitionists-debt-lord-mansfield > Accessed August 2, 2013.

19  Cotter, 32.

20  Fryer, 203.

21  Fryer, 96.

22  Foreman. Kobo Edition.

23  Fryer, 69.

24  Mayhew, Google Books.

25  Fryer, 85.

26  Fryer, 104.

27  Picard, *Dr. Johnson*, 14.

28  Fryer, 234.

29  Benson, 5.

30  Fryer, 235.

31  Fryer, 131.

32  Benson, 5.

33  Gretchen Holbrook Gerzina, editor, *Black Victorians/Black Victoriana.* (New Jersey: Rutgers University Press, 2003), 2.

34  Fryer, 97.


Chapter 10

1  Cruickshank, Kobo edition.

2  Hallie Rubenhold, *Harris's List of Covent-Garden Ladies: Sex in the City in Georgian Britain.* (Great Britain: Tempus Publishing Ltd, 2005), 24.

3  David Nokes. *Jane Austen: A Life* (California: University of California Press, Ltd), 1997.

4  Clive Emsley, Tim Hitchcock and Robert Shoemaker, "Crime and Justice - Crimes Tried at the Old Bailey", Old Bailey Proceedings Online (www.oldbaileyonline.org, version 7.0, 02 February 2014 )

5  Cruickshank, Kobo edition.

6  Mayhew, Google Books.

7  Rubenhold, 37.

8  Rubenhold, 54.

9   Rubenhold, 15.
10  Rubenhold, 32.
11  Rubenhold, 100.
12  Josephine E. Butler, *Personal Reminiscences of a Great Crusade*. (London: H. Marshall & Son, 1910). PDF copy, OpenLibrary.org.
13  Cruickshank, Kobo edition.
14  Upchurch, 187.
15  Graham Robb, *Strangers: Homosexual Love in the Nineteenth Century* (USA: Norton, 2003), 26.
16  Cruickshank, Kobo edition.
17  Rictor Norton, "Mother Clap's Molly House", The Gay Subculture in Georgian England, 5 February 2005 . <http://rictornorton.co.uk/eighteen/mother.htm>.
18  Cruickshank, Kobo edition.
19  Old Bailey Proceedings Online (www.oldbaileyonline.org, version 7.0, 10 February 2014), April 1726, trial of Thomas Wright (t17260420-67).
20  Old Bailey Proceedings Online (www.oldbaileyonline.org, version 7.0, 10 February 2014), April 1726, trial of Gabriel Lawrence (t17260420-64).
21  Cruickshank, Kobo edition.
22  Old Bailey Proceedings Online (www.oldbaileyonline.org, version 7.0, 11 February 2014), July 1726, trial of Margaret Clap (t17260711-54).
23  Cruickshank, Kobo edition.
24  Robert Aldrich and Garry Wotherspoon, *Who's who in Gay and Lesbian History: From Antiquity to World War II*. (New York: Routledge, 2001), 66.
25  Rubenhold, 46-47.
26  Robb, 75.
27  Worsley, 82.
28  Cruickshank, Kobo edition.
29  Cruickshank, Kobo edition.
30  Cruickshank, Kobo edition.

Chapter 11
1   http://www.florence-nightingale.co.uk/ Accessed February 1, 2014.
2   http://www.maryseacole.com/maryseacole/pages/aboutmary2.html Accessed February 1, 2014.
3   Science Museum, <http://www.sciencemuseum.org.uk/ > Accessed February 2, 2014.
4   Goodman, *How to be Victorian*, Kobo edition.
5   The British Library Board, < http://www.bl.uk/learning/histcitizen/georgians/health/hygiene.html > Accessed February 3, 2013.
6   Picard, *Dr. Johnson*, 124.
7   Goodman, *How to be Victorian*, Kobo edition.
8   Caroline Rance, *The Quack Doctor* (Great Britain: The History Press, 2013), Kobo edition.
9   Goodman, *How to be Victorian*, Kobo edition.
10  Aikens, 43.
11  Aikens, 43.

12 Aikens, 43.
13 Picard, *Victorian London*, 72.
14 Carole Rawcliffe, "The Hospitals of Later Medieval London," *Medical History* 28 (1984):1-21.
15 Goodman, *How to be Victorian*, Kobo edition.
16 Charlotte Hodgman. BBC History Magazine, Oct 2012: 76, 77
17 Picard, *Dr. Johnson*, 95.
18 Picard, *Dr. Johnson,* 165.

Chapter 12
1 http://www.eliwhitney.org/museum/eli-whitney/cotton-gin Accessed February 2, 2014.
2 Goodman, *Victorian Farm*, 23.
3 Marilyn Ogilvie and Joy Harvey, *The Biographical Dictionary of Women in Science: Pioneering Lives from Ancient Times to the Mid-20th Century* (London: Routledge, 2000).
4 Picard, *Victorian London*, 34.
5 Richard Conniff. *What the Luddites Really Fought Against.* Smithsonian.com, March 2011.
6 National Geographic, *Concise History,* 160.

# Select Bibliography

A book of this focus and scope can be a tricky thing to organize, in terms of its bibliography and references. If I were to include every single book, magazine, and text I read during the time I've been working on this book, I'd have an entire book of references alone.

I've opted to go with a selected bibliography, listing references cited in this work and also sources that I feel would be useful for further reading and research. All of these references are excellent starting points and I recommend you picking up a few from your local library. Also, places like Project Gutenberg, Archive.Org, and Google Books have a growing selection of digitized copies of once difficult to find books.

Acton, Eliza. *Modern Cookery for Private Families*. London: Longman, Green, Longman, Roberts, and Green, 1864. Digitized by Google Books.

Abbott, Elizabeth. *A History of Mistresses*. Toronto: HarperPerennial, 2004.

Adkins, Roy, and Lesley Adkins. *Jane Austen's England*. New York: Penguin Group (USA), 2013.

Aldrich, Robert and Garry Wotherspoon, *Who's who in Gay and Lesbian History: From Antiquity to World War II*. New York: Routledge, 2001.

Anonymous. *Advice to Governesses*. London: J. Hatchard, 1827.

Anonymous. *The female soldier, or the surprising life and*

*adventures of Hannah Snell.* London, 1750. Digitized by Project Gutenberg.

*At Home With the Georgians.* DVD. Directed by Phil Cairney, Neil Crombie, Iain Scollay. 2010. UK: BBC, 2010.

Austen, Jane. *Emma.* London: John Murray, 1815.

——. *Mansfield Park.* London: Thomas Egerton, 1814.

——. *Pride and Prejudice.* London: T. Egerton, Whitehall, 1813.

August, Andrew. *Poor Women's Lives: Gender, Work, and Poverty in Late-Victorian London.* London: Associated University Press Inc, 1999.

BBC History. < http://www.bbc.co.uk/history/0/ > *See Chapter Notes for specific citations.*

Beeton, Isabella. *The Book of Household Management*, 1861. Digitized by Project Gutenberg.

Benson, Susan. *Ambiguous Ethnicity.* Cambridge University Press. 1981: Great Britain.

Berry, Laura C. *The Child, the State, and the Victorian Novel.* Charlottesville, VA: University Press of Virginia, 1999.

Binny, John and Henry Mayhew. *The Criminal Prisons of London and Scenes of Prison Life.* London: Griffin, Bohn, and Company, 1862.

Bowlby, Chris. "Changing Times: There's more to domestic service than Downton Abbey." BBC History Magazine. Oct 2012

The British Library Board, <http://www.bl.uk/learning/histcitizen/georgians/health/hygiene.html > Accessed February 7, 2014.

British Weekly Commissioners. *Toilers in London: Inquiries Concerning Female Labour in the Metropolis.* London: Hodder and Stoughton, 1889. Digitized by Google Books.

Broomfield, Andrea. *Food and Cooking in Victorian England.* Westpost, CT: Praeger Publishers, 2007.

Butler, Josephine E. *Personal Reminiscences of a Great Crusade.* London: H. Marshall & Son, 1910. PDF copy, OpenLibrary.org.

Chevasse, Pye. *Advice to a wife on the management of herself.*

1875. Digitized by Google Books.

Conniff, Richard. *What the Luddites Really Fought Against*. Smithsonian.com, March 2011.

Cotter, William. *The Somerset Case and the Abolition of Slavery in England*. Oxford: The Historical Association, 1994. PDF from < http://equianosworld.tubmaninstitute.ca >

Cruickshank, Dan. *London's Sinful Secret*. New York: St. Martin's Press, 2009. Kobo edition.

Cullingford, Benita. *British Chimney Sweeps: Give Centuries of Chimney Sweeping*. London: New Amsterdam Books, 2001.

Dickerson, Vanessa A. *Dark Victorians*. University of Illinois Press. 2008.

Eli Whitney Museum and Workshop. <http://www.eliwhitney.org/museum/eli-whitney/cotton-gin> Accessed February 2, 2014.

Fielding, Henry. *Enquiry into the causes of the late increase of robbery*. 1751. Digitized by Google Books.

——.*The History of Tom Jones, a Foundling*. Britain: Andrew Millar, 1749.

Florence Nightingale Museum. < http://www.florence-nightingale.co.uk > Accessed February 1, 2014.

Foreman, Amanda. *The Duchess*. HarperCollins Publishers, 2008. Kobo Edition.

——.*<http://www.amanda-foreman.com/PDFS/ The_Times_How_do_you_solve_a_problem_like_Georgia na.pdf>* Accessed October 2, 2013.

Fryer, Peter. *Staying Power*. New York: PlutoPress, 2010.

Gerzina, Gretchen Holbrook, editor. *Black Victorians/Black Victoriana*. New Jersey: Rutgers University Press, 2003.

Goodman, Ruth. *How to be a Victorian*. London: Penguin Books Ltd, 2013.

Goodman, Ruth, *et al.* (2010). *Victorian Farm: Christmas Edition*. Pavilion: Great Britain.

Halperin, John. *The Life of Jane Austen*. Maryland: The Johns Hopkins University Press, 1984.

Hargrave, Francis. *An Argument in the case of James*

Sommersett, a Negro, wherein it is attempted to demonstrate the present unlawfulness of Domestic Slavery in England. London: 1772. Digitized by Google Books.

Higginbotham, Peter. *Workhouses of the Midlands*. Great Britain: The History Press, 2009.

Houston, Gail T. *Consuming Fictions: Gender, Class, and Hunger in Dickens's Novels*. Carbondale, IL: Southern Illinois University Press, 1994.

Inglis, Lucy. *Georgian London: Into the Streets*. London: Penguin Books Ltd, 2013. Kindle Edition.

Low, Donald. *Thieves' Kitchen: The Regency Underworld*. London: J. M. Dent and Sons Ltd, 1982.

Mary Secole Centre.
<http://www.maryseacole.com/maryseacole/pages/aboutmary2.html > Accessed February 1, 2014.

Mayhew, Henry. *London Labour and the London poor: The London Street-Folk, Vol. 1*. 1861. Digitized by Google Books.

——. *London Labour and the London poor: The London Street-Folk Vol. 2*. 1861. Digitized by Google Books.

——. *London Labour and the London poor: The London Street-Folk, Vol. 3*. 1861. Digitized by Google Books.

——. *London Labour and the London poor: Those that will not work, Vol 4*. 1861. Digitized by Google Books.

Murray, Venetia. *An Elegant Madness: High Society in Regency England*. Great Britain: Penguin Books Ltd, 1998.

The National Archives. http://www.nationalarchives.gov.uk/ *See Chapter Notes for specific entries.*

National Geographic. *National Geographic Concise History of Science and Invention: An Illustrated Time Line*. USA: National Geographic, 2009.

Newton, Judith L., Mary P. Ryan, and Judith R. Walkowitz. *Sex and Class in Women's history*. Great Britain: The Thetford Press Ltd, 1983.

Nokes, David. *Jane Austen: A Life*. California: University of California Press, Ltd, 1997.

Norton, Rector. "Mother Clap's Molly House", The Gay

Subculture in Georgian England, 5 February 2005 <http://rictornorton.co.uk/eighteen/mother.htm>.

——. *Mother Clap's Molly House: The Gay Subculture in England*. London: Nonsuch Publishing, 2007.

Ogilvie, Marilyn and Joy Harvey. *The Biographical Dictionary of Women in Science*. London: Routledge, 2000

Old Bailey Proceedings Online (www.oldbaileyonline.org, version 7.0) 2012-2014. *See Chapter Notes for specific entries.*

Picard, Liza. *Dr. Johnson's London: Life in London 1740-1770*. Great Britain: Weidenfeld & Nicolson. 2000

——. *Victorian London: The Life of a City 1840-1870*. London: Orion Books Ltd, 2005.

Pool, Daniel. *What Jane Austen Ate and Charles Dickens Knew*. New York: Touchstone, 1993.

Probert, Rebecca. "Living in Sin," *BBC History Magazine*, October 2012, 40-43.W.T. Stead Resource Site.

"The Maiden Tribute of Modern Babylon." Accessed September 2, 2013. http://www.attackingthedevil.co.uk/pmg/tribute

Pybus, William. *A Manual of Useful Knowledge*. London: 1810. Digitized by Google Books.

Radcliffe, M. *A Modern System of Domestic Cookery*. 1839. Digitized by Google Books.

Rance, Caroline. *The Quack Doctor*. Great Britain: The History Press, 2013. Kobo edition.

Rawcliffe, Carole. *The Hospitals of Later Medieval London*. Medical History, 1984, 28: 1-21.

Richardson, Ruth. *Dickens and the Workhouse*. Oxford: Oxford University Press, 2012.

Robb, Graham. *Strangers: Homosexual Love in the Nineteenth Century*. USA: Norton, 2003.

The Royal Naval Museum. <http://www.royalnavalmuseum.org/info_sheet_impressm ent.htm> Accessed July 2, 2013.

Rubenhold, Hallie. *Harris's List of Covent-Garden Ladies: Sex in the City in Georgian Britain*. Great Britain: Tempus

Publishing Ltd, 2005.

Rundell, Maria Eliza. *A New System of Domestic Cookery.* London: J. Murray, 1833. Digitized by Google Books.

Sarudy, Barbara Wells. <http://bjws.blogspot.ca/2013/10/hunting-fowling-shooting-in-18c-british.html > Accessed January 16, 2014.

Science Muesum. http://www.sciencemuseum.org.uk/ Accessed February 2, 2014.

Spitalfields Life. <http://spitalfieldslife.com/2010/09/29/the-life-of-a-mudlark-1861/ > Accessed November 20, 2013.

Soyer, Alexis. *The Modern Housewife or Ménagère.* London: Simpskin, Marshall, & Co., 1851. Digitized by Project Gutenberg.

——. *Soyer's Charitable Cookery.* London: 1847. Digitized by Google Books.

Sullivan, Margaret C. *The Jane Austen Handbook.* Philadelphia: Quirk Books, 2007.

Upchurch, Charles. *Before Wilde: Sex Between Men in Britain's Age of Reform.* California: University of California Press, 2009.

Usherwood, Stephen. "The Black Must Be Discharged." *History Today.* <http://www.historytoday.com/stephen-usherwood/black-must-be-discharged-abolitionists-debt-lord-mansfield > Accessed August 2, 2013.

Vickery, Amanda. *The Gentleman's Daughter: Women's Lives in Georgian England.* Yale university press. 1998. New Haven.

——.*Radio 4's A History of Private Life.* AudioGo Ltd, 2010. Audiobook.

*Victorian Farm.* DVD. Directed by Stuart Elliott. UK: Lion Television, 2009.

Walkowitz, Judith R. *City of Dreadful Delight: Narratives of Sexual Danger in Late-Victorian London.* Chicago: The University of Chicago press, 1992.

The War of 1812. <http://www.warof1812.ca/food.htm> The Discriminating General: 1995.

Walsh, John Henry. *A Manual of Domestic Economy*. London: G. Routledge & Co, 1856. Digitized by Google Books.

Wilson, A. N. *The Victorians*. New York: W. W. Norton, 2003.

W.T. Stead Resource Site. "The Maiden Tribute of Modern Babylon." Accessed September 2, 2013. <http://www.attackingthedevil.co.uk/pmg/tribute >

Worsley, Lucy. *If These Walls Could Talk*. New York: Bloomsbury, 2011.

# Author Biography

Canadian author Krista D. Ball combines her love of the fantastical, an obsession with Jane Austen, and a history degree from Mount Allison University to bring both writers and muslin lovers a new and unique reference guide.

Krista was born and raised in Newfoundland, where she learned how to use a chainsaw, chop wood, and make raspberry jam. She lives in Alberta these days. Somehow, she's picked up an engineer, two kids, six cats, and a very understanding corgi off ebay. Her credit card has been since taken away. You can find her causing trouble at http://kristadball.com

# ALSO FROM TYCHE BOOKS

If you loved Hustlers, Harlots and Heroes, don't miss Krista's first book of the series!

What Kings Ate
and Wizards Drank
by
Krista D. Ball

Equal parts writer's guide, comedy, and historical cookbook, fantasy author Krista D. Ball takes readers on a journey into the depths of epic fantasy's obsession with rabbit stew., how to move armies across enemy territories without starving to death, and what a medieval pantry should look like when your heroine is seducing the hero.

Steam and Stratagem
by
Christopher Hoare

Welcome to the Steampunk World of Regency...

Roberta Stephenson is the daughter of the 'Father of Railways', a girl almost raised in the engine works, and further educated in the most advanced halls of Miss Mather's Academy for Girls. Now, she wants to become manager and designer at her father's steamship yard on the Clyde.

And Britain needs Roberta's expertise, for her steam powered battering rams may be the only thing that can stop Napoleon's latest invasion plan.

# WWW.TYCHEBOOKS.COM

# ALSO FROM TYCHE BOOKS

### Tantamount
### by
### Thomas J. Radford

Trained to fight, lead, and sail the ocean that is space, Nel Vaughn has the makings of a hero. She should have been the best, but Nel forsake a career with the Alliance and now sails the Free Lanes on the Tantamount with its misfit crew, Kitsune cabin girl, and absent-minded captain.

During a stopover for repairs, Nel and the Tantamount are coerced into a mission that will challenge Nel's simple goal of keeping her ship intact and her crew safe . . . unless Nel chooses to be the hero she was meant to be.

### Blightcross
### by
### C. A. Lang

For fugitive soldier and thief Capra Jorassian, the city-state of Blightcross is an opportunity to earn enough money for her freedom. Stealing an enchanted painting from the dictator's collection is nothing new. But the simple heist gets complicated quickly when Capra's childhood friend shows up, bent on bringing her back for court martial. Then her eccentric employer, the creator of the painting, is kidnapped, throwing Capra into a struggle for the survival of Blightcross, with only her enemies as allies.

# WWW.TYCHEBOOKS.COM

CPSIA information can be obtained at www.ICGtesting.com
Printed in the USA
LVOW07s2343110414

381380LV00003B/15/P